D

Liberalism

John Hoffman

Advanced
Topic*Master*

Series editor
Eric Magee

Philip Allan Updates
Market Place
Deddington
Oxfordshire
OX15 0SE

Orders
Bookpoint Ltd, 130 Milton Park, Abingdon, Oxfordshire, OX14 4SB
tel: 01235 827720
fax: 01235 400454
e-mail: uk.orders@bookpoint.co.uk
Lines are open 9.00 a.m.–5.00 p.m., Monday to Saturday, with a 24-hour message answering service. You can also order through the Philip Allan Updates website:
www.philipallan.co.uk

Printed in Spain

Environmental information
The paper on which this title is printed is sourced from mills using wood from managed, sustainable forests.

Contents

Conclusion

Introduction

Liberalism can be difficult to examine because it is so influential and differentiated. Often fierce battles are conducted between different wings of the liberal tradition, and liberalism differs according to the national context in which it occurs.

In the UK today, for example, it is not only the Liberal Democratic Party who are liberals. In fact, liberalism, when defined as a set of values that stresses the importance of individual freedom and toleration, can be found in most political parties, even though these parties differ in their economic, social and environmental policies. 'We are all liberals now' has been the position of societies in Europe (and parts of Asia, Africa and the Americas) for a long time, and it could be argued that the collapse of the communist states in eastern Europe has seen the prestige of liberalism rise even further.

Diversity and definition

One writer, Fukuyama, has even proclaimed that history has come to an end with the development of liberal capitalism, although many liberals disagree with this. Nevertheless, it is true to say that the widespread support for liberal values makes liberalism difficult to tie down, since if virtually everyone is a liberal, then what does the term mean? How can liberalism be concerned with freedom yet also concerned with order?

The proposal to introduce identity cards in the UK, for example, can be challenged in terms of liberal values, but it can also be championed in terms of these values — how, it is argued, can people be free unless they are also secure? Restrictions on the right to smoke can be castigated as a form of 'health fascism' that erodes the right of the individual; they can also be defended as a way of protecting the health of those who cannot be free if they become more likely to contract lung cancer. Liberalism seems able to point in contradictory directions at the same time, and this makes it difficult to pin down and define.

The national context

The ideology differs according to national contexts, both in the form it takes and the term used to describe it. In the USA the word 'liberalism' denotes views close to social democracy elsewhere. No self-respecting free marketeer in the USA would call himself or herself a liberal!

In the UK the word preserves its full ambiguity, so that the revival of free-market doctrines associated with the policies of Margaret Thatcher (1925–) is termed liberalism or neoliberalism, even though such liberalism is different from the liberalism of the Liberal Democrats. Liberalism in Europe often has a social dimension that makes it close to social democracy, while in the new Russia a party led by Vladimir Zhirinovsky (1946–), which has extreme, right-wing, nationalist policies, calls itself the Liberal Democratic Party!

The relationship to socialism

Liberalism is associated with capitalism, but it can be close to socialism too — democratic socialism was memorably described by Eduard Bernstein (1850–1932) as 'organising liberalism'. Liberalism can be anti-communist to the extent that it treats communists and socialists as enemies of state (as occurred during the McCarthyism period in the USA); it can also be so close to communism that doctrines like Eurocommunism have sometimes been described as communism with a liberal face.

Its view of the market differs accordingly. On the one hand, liberalism may extol the market mechanism as central to autonomy and freedom; on the other hand, it may see the market as an institution that requires considerable regulation by the state. The welfare state is regarded by some liberals as an almost totalitarian institution, yet it can be praised by others as the embodiment of liberal values.

Doctrine and ideology

Liberals pride themselves on being open-minded and practical, and, understandably, resent the idea that they are subscribing to a doctrine or an ideology.

But is liberalism a doctrine? A doctrine has been defined as 'a strongly held single view or collection of connected views'. Adherents to liberalism feel uneasy about this label since the word 'doctrinaire' is seen as the antithesis of open-mindedness and toleration. Yet liberalism is certainly a doctrine, albeit one that is interpreted by its followers in radically different ways; all liberals share a 'strong' belief in freedom and the individual.

Since an ideology is simply a set of beliefs outlining a desirable vision of a society, there is no reason why liberalism should not be described as an ideology too. Doctrines are sometimes seen as less comprehensive than ideologies, but, like doctrines, ideologies can be dogmatic and rigid, although in my view dogmatism is not a defining property of an ideology per se. Liberalism is certainly an ideology, espousing the rights of the individual, freedom, toleration and a respect for difference, however differently these values may be interpreted.

John Hoffman

Acknowledgements

I am grateful to Eric Magee for his help and advice. I have found that writing for and editing *Politics Review* has been a huge help in writing this work. Philip Allan Updates has been a wonderful publisher to work for, and I hope that our association will long continue.

I am grateful to Edinburgh University Press for permission to draw upon work that I have done for *Glossary of Political Theory*.

Rowan Roenisch has been encouraging and helpful, as have my daughter, Frieda Roenisch, and my son, Fred Hoffman.

Chapter 1

Liberalism or liberalisms?

The subversion of natural hierarchy

The earliest political thinkers that we have record of — the ancient Greeks — saw hierarchy as natural and therefore, in Aristotle's celebrated dictum, defined the state itself as belonging to a class of objects that exist in nature. Humans are divided by nature into citizens and slaves, and this particularist view makes liberalism impossible. Liberals, by contrast, see the state as artificial — human-made — and, as we shall see, they have considerable difficulty arguing why people should obey the state. The point is that no liberal can argue that it is natural for some people to have rights while others do not. This notion is in stark contrast to ancient and medieval views.

The ancient Greeks are famous for treating people in concrete terms. People play specific social and political roles: they do not exist simply as 'individuals'. It has been said that the concept of the individual 'is a tiresome modern abstraction which is almost designed to mislead': this 'obfuscating' notion hardly appears in antiquity, and can scarcely be expressed in Ancient Greek, or, for that matter, Latin. As Hegel was fond of saying, the ancient Greeks did not know 'man as such'.

The sophists

It is true, however, that the ancient Greek sophists have been described as the liberals of the ancient world. Hobbes, Locke and Rousseau (all, in my view, classical liberals) are sometimes cited as 'the modern representatives' of the sophistic tradition. The sophists were educators who travelled widely and developed a sceptical and individualist position that saw nature and law at loggerheads with one another. Like modern liberals, they saw the state as artificial or (as it is usually called) conventional in character.

While this view contrasted sharply with Plato and Aristotle's position that the state is natural in character, the argument that the sophists were early liberals needs to be approached with caution. Protagoras, often seen as a champion of political equality, saw the state as a divinely sanctioned institution (certainly not a liberal view), while other sophists (as Plato points out) equated might with right. Antiphon takes the view that the state should be evaded wherever possible, and, unsurprisingly, he has been characterised as an antisocial thinker unable to accept that people have to live together.

Liberalism does not only accept that the state is artificial. It seeks to find a way in which natural freedoms can be preserved through institutions of a social and political kind. It is concerned with order and government, so the sophistic notion of nature is similar to that of classical liberalism, but there the similarity ends.

Hobbes and the state of nature

Classical liberals argued that because people are naturally free and equal, it is logical to depict them as first living in a state of nature. The most famous exponent of this notion was the English liberal, Thomas Hobbes (1588–1679). (Note that the designation of Hobbes as a liberal is controversial, as we shall see.)

Hobbes directly contrasts his position with Aristotle and argues that, while bees and ants might live sociably among one another, the same is not true of humans. People compete around notions of honour and dignity in a world in which one person's gain is another's loss. Every person puts their self-interest first, and this leads to a world of war and strife. Peace, trade, culture and industry are impossible according to Hobbes — his state of nature is a war of all against all.

Thomas Hobbes

This is in sharp contrast with the ancient Greek view that humans are naturally sociable and live by nature in a state. It conflicts with the medieval view as well. Although medieval writers like Aquinas (1224–74) were committed as Christians to a belief in equality, since every human being is created by a common divinity, this egalitarianism is confined to our existence before the Fall. Once Adam and Eve were expelled from Eden, humans were corrupted by nature and sin ('the mother of servitude'), and thus, for medieval Christians as well as for ancient Greeks and Romans, people divide into citizens and slaves, men and women etc., in the time-honoured way. Nature becomes a source of timeless hierarchy and repression.

Hobbes not only rejects medievalism — he is no sophist either, since his construct of a turbulent state of nature is intended to make the case for a state. People are competitive and egotistic. That is how they are made by God. Religion plays a vital role in his theory; Hobbes was attacked as an atheist, and he certainly upset some conservatives by arguing that the church itself must be brought under the control of a sovereign state. He was a believer in a strong state, certainly, but his assumptions are basically liberal. People are free and equal by *nature*. Self-interested as they are, people are also rational and, Hobbes believes, can see that the formation of a sovereign state is in their interests. What Hobbes calls a 'Common Power' keeps people in awe and directs their actions to the 'Common Benefit'. The 'Common Power' is the sovereign state, while the 'Common Benefit' refers to the interests of all.

How is the state envisaged by Hobbes formed? Because everyone is free and equal, they must consent to be ruled. After all, the state is merely the power of the individual writ large: the state re-presents (or represents) the God-given sovereignty of the individual in collective form. By agreement or 'covenant' people authorise a sovereign (who may be an individual or an assembly) and they keep only their natural right to self-preservation. All other natural rights are yielded to their sovereign, who as a kind of 'moral god' provides peace and security in return.

This is an astonishing argument. On the one hand, it appears authoritarian in that it allows the sovereign unlimited power. On the other hand, it rests on the assumption that all rule must be authorised — people have to consent to government. Although, as we shall see, it is anachronistic to call this argument democratic, it lies at the heart of the liberal argument that people are 'born free' and can only be governed by laws that they have approved.

Locke's 'inconveniences'

John Locke (1632–1704) based his case for civil government upon a more agreeable version of the state of nature. Like Hobbes, he too begins with the assumption that humans initially inhabit a state of 'perfect freedom' and equality in which they are able to live their lives as they see fit.

In both Hobbes and Locke's state of nature, there is no state — no institution claiming a monopoly of legitimate force (in Max Weber's famous definition) — and individuals are deemed separate from one another. However, in Locke's state of nature, people act in accordance with the laws of nature and behave in a relatively orderly fashion — in fact, so much so that some anarchists argue for a stateless society based on a Lockean state of nature. One might well ask why, if people can order their lives in this 'natural' way, is a state necessary at all?

Locke's argument is that 'inconveniences' increase in this situation, making a contract necessary to establish a legitimate state. When a person mixes his/her labour with an object, it becomes his/her property. Although initially people are entitled to own only what they can use, the invention of money makes it possible to store and accumulate wealth, and with the division of society into rich and poor, violent conflicts are generated. This is linked to Locke's argument that people become increasingly unable to defend their interests through interpreting the laws of nature in an acceptable way, and with flagrant partisanship the need for a body that aspires to impartiality and commands consent becomes increasingly acute. A state is necessary that can make laws, and Locke allows for a right to revolution where the state acts in a despotic way, interfering with property and personal rights.

It was Locke's variant of the state of nature thesis that inspired American colonists about a century later to rebel against the British Crown on the basis that their natural rights to be governed with consent and representation had been violated.

Rousseau and inequality

Jean-Jacques Rousseau (1712–78) is the last of the classical liberals to rely upon the notion of a state of nature and to base the state upon a social contract (note that, like Hobbes, his liberal credentials are controversial). In Rousseau's view, both Hobbes and Locke are guilty of anachronism (the latter allows individuals in the state of nature to consent to the use of money). They regard as 'natural' people who are in fact merely the 'possessive individuals' of the seventeenth century.

Jean-Jacques Rousseau

Rousseau argues for a state of nature in which people are animal-like in their simplicity and attitudes. But although they are mostly governed by instincts, they have an attribute that sets them apart from other animals. This is their capacity for free will, or, as Rousseau puts it, 'free agency'. Like the inhabitants of Hobbes and Locke's state of nature, people are separate individuals who have chance encounters with other individuals, and they govern themselves as abstract individuals: they have no relationships with other people.

This leads Rousseau to argue that civilisation is a force for corruption, and that property, crucial to Locke's notion of natural rights, has in fact spawned 'crimes, wars and murders'. The discovery of corn and iron may have civilised 'man', but it has ruined humanity. The acquisitive drives deemed natural by Hobbes and Locke are seen as the products of civilisation by Rousseau. These drives are themselves the artificial products of an unequal and divided society.

Reason, which is seen as a natural God-given attribute by Hobbes and Locke, enables us, as far as Rousseau is concerned, to justify in hypocritical fashion division and inequality. Rousseau makes a sharp distinction between fraudulent social contracts, in which the rich have used contractual arguments to prettify their exploitation of the poor, and a genuine social contract able to secure legitimacy and equality, and which embodies rather than perverts natural freedom.

In Rousseau's social contract everybody gives up everything in such a way that a new entity is created — the legitimate state, based upon a general will and a communal identity. For this reason, many commentators do not see Rousseau as liberal, but as a socialist and even a totalitarian. But this view, I think, is mistaken. Rousseau bases his whole theory upon the individual (conceived as a self-contained atom) and, despite his critique of inequality, he is still wedded to the classical liberal view that all humans have a desire for private property which nothing can change.

The notion of a general will implies that society is more than the sum of its parts, and Rousseau argues that the rights of the individual must give way to the 'right of the community over everything'. But his comment that the general will — which embodies the will of the whole people — can force the individual to be free, is no more than a graphic description of the liberal justification of the state. Rousseau argues that force is a physical power (he said 'I do not see how its effects could produce morality'), but if this makes the state an institution that claims to use force morally, this is paradoxically a problem that affects the whole of the liberal tradition. The state is authorised by individuals to use force against them. It is not simply Rousseau's problem alone. Rousseau, it might be said,

takes the contradiction between force and freedom by the horns, and exposes it for all to see.

Table 1.1 Classical liberalism and the state of nature

Author	View of the state of nature	Ideological implication
Hobbes	the war of all against all	an authoritarian state
Locke	'inconveniences' in enforcing the law of nature	a liberal representative state
Rousseau	inequality brought about by civilisation and property	participation in making laws in a communal state

The attack on natural rights: Hume and Burke

After Rousseau, the notion of the social contract, in which people leave a state of nature and rationally decide to form a state, was abandoned. David Hume (1711–76) takes the view that the state arises through habit rather than contract. It could be argued that abandoning the notion of a state of nature is positive, since it is grotesque to imagine humans living as isolated individuals without social relationships. However, the greater realism of Hume is accompanied by his uncritical view that force is employed in a concentrated form in the earliest societies, and in place of natural rights is substituted by what he calls a 'sensible utility'. Hume defends the need for limited government, general and uniform laws and the pursuit of commerce.

Hume was sceptical that rights exist in nature, and in this he was followed by Edmund Burke (1729–97), who fiercely attacked the natural rights philosophy of the French revolutionaries (defended in Britain by writers like Paine). Burke developed a form of conservatism in which, as Gray has commented in his book *Liberalism* (1986), 'liberal values are preserved but liberal hopes chastened'.

Hume greatly influenced the Scottish Enlightenment — a tradition that also rejects social contract theory — and the economist Adam Smith (1723–90), who sees humans as naturally social, charting the development of humanity from hunting, pasturage and agriculture, and culminating in commerce. 'Natural liberty' is associated with the innate tendency in humans to truck and barter, and the liberal state, with its general laws and social neutrality, reflects human nature and laws of justice.

Utilitarianism

Utilitarians, such as Jeremy Bentham (1748–1832) and James Mill (1773–1836), reject the notion of natural rights as a 'nonsense on stilts' and contend that all humans are dominated by drives that lead them to pursue pleasure and avoid pain.

But it is not plausible to argue, as Gray does, that Bentham and Mill began a rupture with the liberal tradition, for their work develops out of the critique of classical liberalism developed by Hume and the Scottish Enlightenment. Like the classical liberals, utilitarians hold that individuals are governed by natural drives, and James Mill finds Hobbes a thinker whose logic is difficult to 'controvert'. It is true that the utilitarians rejected 'the anarchical fallacies' of the classical tradition (i.e. the theory of natural rights), but their view of the state and society is quintessentially liberal in character.

The problem of minority rights

Liberals, however, were to become aware of a problem with Benthamite utilitarianism. The greatest happiness of the greatest number could be secured through majoritarian measures of an illiberal character, and this meant that the pursuit of pleasure and the avoidance of pain might lead to intolerance and the oppression of minorities.

As L. T. Hobhouse (1864–1929) complained, might not a 'wise despot' pursue policies that maximise the happiness of the greatest number? Even if the formal apparatus is democratic, is it not possible that a majority, say, of tea drinkers might oppress a minority who prefer wine?

John Stuart Mill (1806–73) undertook to modify Bentham's argument. In his *Utilitarianism* (1861) he argues for a qualified view of pleasure, suggesting that higher pleasures (like poetry) are more valuable than lower pleasures (like push-pin, a Victorian version of pinball), on the grounds that those who experience both always opt for the former over the latter. The point about Mill's argument is that he forgoes, as he puts it, 'any advantage which could be derived to my argument from the idea of abstract right, as a thing independent of utility'. He regards utility as 'the ultimate appeal on all questions; but it must be utility in the largest sense, grounded on the permanent interests of a man as a progressive being'.

The emphasis on progress and change enables Mill to extend liberalism to groups that he feels have been excluded by traditional argument: women and the poor. Hobhouse was to argue that Mill spans 'the interval between the old

and New Liberalism', and this transition certainly demonstrates that fierce debate can occur between different wings of the liberal tradition.

John Stuart Mill

Mill's critique of the utilitarianism of Bentham and James Mill was accompanied by an attempt to reconstruct liberalism so that it was better able to handle social problems. Although Gray (1995) argues that John Stuart Mill engineered 'a decisive breach in the intellectual fabric of the liberal tradition', in fact Mill built upon and extended the individualism of the past.

John Stuart Mill

His argument in *On Liberty* (1859) is that the question of freedom is posed in new conditions and needs to face up to the problem which the majority might pose for individual liberties. Liberals in the past defended the freedom of the individual against a minority of feudal-minded autocrats; now they had to defend the individual against (if necessary) a majority of 'the people'.

Mill champions the need for toleration, arguing that more precise criteria are needed to establish the boundaries between legitimate and illegitimate social intervention, whether this takes the form of law or public opinion. His celebrated 'harm principle' basically argues that when an individual's action is self-regarding — i.e. it only pertains to the individual's own interests — it should be tolerated, and intervention is only justified when an action affects others.

Natural penalties and the problem of slavery

Of course, as contemporary criticism and subsequent commentary have demonstrated, Mill's argument is anything but the 'very simple principle' Mill claimed it to be. It is clear that Mill is not denying that everything one individual does affects another, but he is making a distinction between affecting others and affecting *their interests*. If I am religious, then the existence of an atheist might upset me, but unless the atheist prevents me from worshipping as I wish, then he or she cannot be said to affect my interests.

Nor is Mill, in my view, arguing that individuals can do what they like to themselves, although he does imply this when he says that 'each is the proper guardian of their health, whether bodily, *or* mental and spiritual'. In the first place, a person can through 'advice, instruction, persuasion and avoidance' express their disapproval of another's self-regarding activities. Indeed, a person may suffer 'very severe penalties at the hands of others for faults which directly concern only himself', but these penalties (which Mill calls 'natural') are not, strictly speaking, punishments. They arise because everything we do affects everyone else; natural penalties (as opposed to deliberate punishments) are 'the spontaneous consequences of the faults themselves'. We cannot stop the atheist from having beliefs of which we disapprove, but we don't have to have coffee with them!

Second, and even more fundamentally, Mill assumes that self-regarding actions are not self-destructive. He makes clear in his chapter of 'Applications' that 'the principle of freedom cannot require that he should be free not to be free'. Supposing, for some bizarre reason, you wished to sell yourself into slavery. This is not a self-regarding action since it is impossible, once it has been undertaken, to exercise a liberty of retraction and change your mind. Such an action would defeat the purpose of freedom.

This point opens up space for social regulation of all acts that infringe the liberty of retraction, whether this regulation involves the imposition of seat belts, restrictions on smoking, or health and safety legislation. You are only entitled to harm yourself when you can recover from such harm: you cannot be free not to be free, since it is not freedom to alienate your freedom. You can only have the right to commit suicide if having tried suicide you can change your mind, and decide to go on living. Classical liberals like Locke had assumed that as an individual made by God, you cannot offend your creator: Mill secularises the argument but preserves the view that you are only sovereign to be sovereign.

In *On Liberty* Mill extends the concept of 'coercion' to embrace the force of public opinion, and in other works he expresses the view that capitalism is unfair to workers as individuals when it rewards disagreeable work with low pay. In *Principles of Political Economy* (1848) he argues that 'the generality of labourers' have as little choice of occupation and freedom of movement, and are as dependent upon fixed rules and the will of others, as they could be in any system 'short of slavery'. Mill extends the notion of individuality not only to workers, but to women as well, and his *Subjection of Women* (which he wrote with Harriet Taylor) is rightly regarded as a seminal text in 'liberal feminism'.

The social liberals: Green and Hobhouse

New liberals, like Green (1836–82) and Hobhouse, accept the case for trade unions, sanitary and health acts, land and tax reform, unemployment and accident insurance, and the policies they advocate generally seek a more equitable distribution of wealth in society at large. Mill had already said that 'a government cannot have too much of the kind of activity which does not impede, but aids and stimulates, individual exertion and development', and the new liberals took the view that the state must provide conditions that maximise the freedom of those who cannot cope on their own.

Hobhouse is happy for liberals to have a dialogue with socialists, and for liberals to adopt socialist policies that strengthen individual freedom. New liberals embrace what has come to be called 'positive freedom': the view that individuals can only be held to be free when they have the means to act in an autonomous way. Freedom of speech, for example, would be deemed meaningless if you didn't have the confidence and knowledge to articulate your views.

Just as Mill had broadened the concept of coercion to take account of unintended but oppressive expressions of public opinion, so Hobhouse speaks of the 'tyranny of circumstance'. Thus an employer, for example, who causes anguish to an employee by making the latter redundant, can be acting tyrannically even if there is no such intention in their action. It is hardly surprising that the architect of the British National Health Service, Sir William Beveridge (1879–1963), was a new liberal.

Neoliberalism and the classical liberal tradition

The 'neoliberalism' associated with the doctrines of Friedrich von Hayek (1899–1992) and Thatcher represents a reaction to the 'socialistic' character of (among other ideologies) new liberalism. The distinction between negative and positive freedom — between freedom *from* and freedom *to* — is, in my view, a reaction against the way liberalism developed into a social creed.

Classical liberals took it for granted that the people whose interests they championed had the power to act: what these individuals needed was the right and space to exercise this power. The idea that freedom is not about power, but about a freedom from deliberately intended interference, is a modern invention projected by those who have reacted against the extension of liberal values to the wrong kind of person: people who require help and assistance from the government if they are to be free. Hayek's notion that we can be free to starve, to make costly mistakes or run mortal risks is not a reversion to classical liberalism, but a new doctrine.

It is true that classical liberalism assumed that free people were materially comfortable, but classical liberals would never have described a starving person as 'free'. As we shall see in Chapter 3, which deals with liberalism and democracy, classical liberals regard the mass of the population as beyond the liberal pale — not part of 'the people'. Neoliberalism is a reaction against social liberalism, resisting fiercely the attempt of the latter to extend liberal values to the poor, women, the disabled etc.

Rawls vs Nozick

Social liberalism has enjoyed a revival in the work of John Rawls (1921–2002) who, in his celebrated *Theory of Justice*, seeks to posit a version of the social contract in which people exist in an 'original position', not knowing their financial situation, 'race', creed, religion or state of health. From this 'veil of ignorance' a theory of justice can emerge which is impartial and authentically universal.

Its first principle embodies freedoms of speech, assembly and to vote, and the right to stand as a representative. This principle is absolute but coexists with a second principle that allows for economic and social inequalities only when the latter benefit society itself. Thus, a doctor can be paid more than a docker since society would suffer if salaries to doctors were lowered, but the inequality between a rich person and a poor person is not justifiable: hence the latter can be taxed more heavily since society gains as a result.

Rawls's social-democratic version of liberalism has been severely criticised by writers like Robert Nozick (1938–2002), whose *Anarchy, State and Utopia* defends the neoliberal view that people are entitled to keep what they have gained lawfully and through good fortune and skill. In his later work *Political Liberalism*, Rawls seeks to argue that people can agree on his theory of justice even though they hold different religious and philosophical views (or conceptions of the good). The point is that debates about liberalism and within liberalism continue, thus demonstrating the heterogeneity of the tradition, even though a definition of a broad kind is possible.

| Table 1.2 | Comparison of three strands of liberalism | | |

Classical liberalism	New liberalism	Neoliberalism
Individuals live in a state of nature	Individuals are social	Individuals are social
State based on consent	State rooted in habit	State rooted in habit
Freedom: negative but the individual takes positive freedom for granted	Freedom: negative and positive	Freedom: negative
Coercion opposed to freedom	Coercion can be compatible with freedom	Coercion opposed to freedom
Democracy not an issue	State must be democratic	State can be democratic if it protects the free market

Core values of liberalism

Although it is possible to distinguish between various kinds of liberalism, they have a number of common features:

- Liberalism is distinctively modern and therefore rejects all ancient and medieval views that see people as playing different roles in a hierarchical community.
- Liberalism focuses on the individual. People are rational and capable of governing their own lives.
- The state is necessary but its right to use force must be agreed by individuals.
- All individuals enjoy the same moral status.
- Every individual is free and equal.
- The individual is a universal idea. All people throughout the world exist as individuals.
- All individuals are capable of improving their lives. They can become more rational, free, equal and moral.

Conclusion

Liberalism espouses the freedom and equality of the individual. In this it breaks dramatically from ancient and medieval views that see people as naturally divided and playing specific roles.

Classical liberals believed that individuals could be conceptualised as living in a state of nature. In Hobbes's view this state of nature is self-destructive, whereas for Locke the state of nature is relatively orderly and is governed by a law of nature. In Rousseau's variant, humans are like animals, although they are able to reason and have free will. Later liberals rejected the notion of a state of nature and the idea that the state was the product of a contract.

Members of the Scottish Enlightenment argue that humans are inherently social, and utilitarians take the view that all individuals are governed by a desire to pursue pleasure and avoid pain. John Stuart Mill modifies classical utilitarianism, and writers like Hobhouse establish a new liberalism that is sympathetic to state regulation and trade unionism. Neoliberalism seeks to return to the idea of an autonomous market, but sharply separates freedom from a view of equality that might generate notions of social justice.

Summary

- What makes liberalism significant historically is its rejection of ancient and medieval notions of a natural and repressive hierarchy. Liberals see the state as artificial and conventional. Although the sophists of the ancient world believed that individuals were free and equal, they were not concerned with constructing a state in which natural freedoms could be preserved.

- Hobbes can be called a classical liberal, because he believes that people inhabit a state of nature and form a state through a social contract. For Hobbes, this state of nature is self-destructive — a war of all against all — and vesting power in the hands of a powerful, sovereign state will bring about peace and order.

- Locke is a classical liberal too, but his state of nature is relatively peaceful and everyone seeks to implement a law of nature. However, with the invention of money this implementation became more and more distorted, and a state representing the interests of all property owners is necessary.

- Rousseau can also be described as a classical liberal, even though his notion of the state of nature is strikingly different to that of Hobbes and Locke. Rousseau believes that everyone must give up everything if the state is to be legitimate, and citizens are part of a community governed by their 'general will'.

- Hume and Burke are the first liberals to reject the idea that everyone has natural rights and that the state is the product of a contract.

- Utilitarians like Bentham and James Mill argue that individuals all have the same interest — the pursuit of pleasure and the avoidance of pain. If all pursue pleasure, this will result in the greatest happiness of the greatest number. Critics of utilitarianism fear that this could result in the suppression of minority tastes and interests.

- John Stuart Mill defends freedom in his classical work *On Liberty*. He argues the case for toleration, insisting that everyone counts, and that freedom can be threatened by intolerant public opinion as well as by unjust laws. Mill opens the way for social liberals like Hobhouse

and Green, who see a positive role for the state in alleviating poverty and regulating the market.

- Social liberalism has been fiercely rejected by neoliberals like Hayek who oppose intervention in the market and take the view that freedom should always be negative in character. This debate has been reflected in the views of Rawls, who espouses a social liberal case for the welfare state, and Nozick, who argues that individuals have the right to govern their lives without state interference in what they acquire and own.

Task 1.1

Read the passage below and answer the questions that follow.

Thomas Hobbes: liberal or authoritarian?

Hobbes lived in a time of upheaval, more dramatic than any England has known since. The country was deeply divided: between rich and poor, between parliament and king. Society was split religiously, economically and regionally. Inequalities in wealth were huge, and the upheavals of the Civil War (1642–51) meant radical religious and political sects proliferated, including the Levellers (who wanted much greater equality in terms of wealth and political rights) and the Diggers (who adopted an early socialist programme seeking the abolition of wage labour.) The country was divided militarily, while the union with Scotland was fragile at best and almost destroyed by King Charles I's attempts to impose consistency in religious practices. Hobbes's greatest fear was social and political chaos — and he had ample opportunity both to observe it and to suffer its effects.

In *The Elements of Law* (1640) Hobbes supported the king against his challengers. Indeed, in France Hobbes served as mathematics tutor to the young, fugitive prince who would later become King Charles II. But although Hobbes backed the monarchy, once the head of King Charles I fell he regarded all rebellion against Parliament as illegitimate. For Hobbes, what is essential is a strong state, able to secure order and protect its inhabitants. Accused of being a turncoat by royalist exiles in France, Hobbes returned to England soon after the publication of *Leviathan* (1651) and presented himself before the Council of State.

Was Hobbes an autocrat? Rousseau speaks bitterly of Hobbes dividing the human species into so many herds of cattle, 'each with its ruler, who keeps guard over them for the purpose of devouring them.' It is true that Hobbes believed the sovereign has far-reaching power, and he describes the sovereign as a 'mortal god', able to promote peace at home and abroad as the sovereign thinks fit. But this does not make him authoritarian or totalitarian.

First, Hobbes argued that the power of the sovereign has to be authorised. Power derives from consent. When a Commonwealth is established by conquest, one might

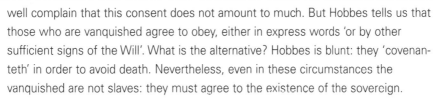

Task 1.1 (continued)

well complain that this consent does not amount to much. But Hobbes tells us that those who are vanquished agree to obey, either in express words 'or by other sufficient signs of the Will'. What is the alternative? Hobbes is blunt: they 'covenanteth' in order to avoid death. Nevertheless, even in these circumstances the vanquished are not slaves: they must agree to the existence of the sovereign.

Second, every individual is naturally equal to every other, the weakest having strength enough to kill the strongest. They give all their rights to their sovereign representative, bar one: the right to self-preservation. This is crucial, for it means, as Hobbes points out, that if a sovereign commands a man to put his life in jeopardy, the individual has the liberty to disobey. If our refusal frustrates the end 'for which the Soveraignty was ordained, then there is no Liberty to refuse: otherwise there is.' Not only is obedience to the sovereign conditional on the individual's absolute right to self-preservation, Hobbes also takes the view that there are few so foolish that they would not rather govern themselves than be governed by others. At the heart of Hobbes's theory is the idea that all individuals are free, equal and able to govern their own lives.

As Leo Strauss points out in his book, *Natural Right and History*, ironically it is Hobbes rather than Locke who stresses most strongly 'the individual's right to resist society or government whenever his self-preservation is threatened.' Who argues that (male) individuals are duty-bound to fight for the state? It is Locke rather than Hobbes. Unsurprisingly, although royalists welcomed Hobbes's support they did not like his ideas. Despite his belief in a strong state, Hobbes can justly be described as the founder of liberalism.

Questions

1 'Hobbes was too authoritarian to be considered a liberal'. Discuss.
2 What role does Hobbes allocate for consent in his theory?
3 Why does Hobbes insist that every individual has the right to self-preservation?
4 Is Hobbes a rationalist?
5 What is Hobbes's view of 'nature'?

Guidance

Question 1

Note that Hobbes allows the sovereign far more power than later liberals would find acceptable. Indeed, it could be argued that Hobbes's sovereign has absolute power: he can do as he pleases. Hobbes was concerned that no limitations should be placed upon the sovereign's power to bring about order. Unlike medieval rulers, the sovereign is not restricted by natural and divine law — in fact, Hobbes argues that what is acceptable in terms of people's beliefs and institutions depends upon the sovereign's wishes.

Task 1.1 (continued)

But this does not make Hobbes an authoritarian or totalitarian. The sovereign *represents* the individual. It is because individuals have absolute power over their own lives that the sovereign has absolute power over all individuals. Each individual is free and equal to every other — even if this is the negative freedom to kill others who threaten you, and all are equal in the sense that each has the strength to do so. No authoritarian or totalitarian would base their power on the freedom and equality of every individual. These are liberal assumptions and explain why Hobbes, though a conservative, was never trusted by the royalists.

Question 2

People leave the state of nature because they agree to do so. The formation of the state usually results from a *contract*. Although this state is much less accountable than later liberals would find acceptable, it has to be authorised — i.e. it rests upon consent — and this is a liberal assumption. It is important to note here that for Hobbes the state is artificial, not natural, in character.

It is true that Hobbes also allows for a state to be formed through conquest, but even here he insists that the conquered inhabitants must indicate their agreement with the conquerors. Their rule is authorised. It might be objected that in reality people do not have much choice, but it is crucial for Hobbes that individuals must consent to their rulers. After all, as indicated in question (a), these rulers are representatives, so when obeying a sovereign individuals are only obeying themselves in a collective form.

Question 3

Hobbes was accused of being an atheist, because he spoke of the state as a mortal god and insisted that every church falls under the power of the state. Yet Hobbes insists that people are made by a creator, and their creator has ensured that every individual has one right nothing can take away — the right to self-preservation.

This means that, no matter how powerful the state, the individual can disobey the law where such a person feels it would threaten his/her self-preservation. This is a liberal assumption, and it flows from Hobbes's view that the state cannot do to the individual what the individual would not do to him or herself. Hobbes assumes that no individual would take his or her own life, and therefore it follows that no state can put the life of the individual in jeopardy. This means that should the state try to execute an individual, the individual can try to evade capture, since such an act by the state would place the individual back into a state of nature and dissolve the sovereign character of the state. Serious punishment is a real problem for Hobbes; while on the one hand the state has the right to punish law-breakers, on the other they are individuals whose right to self-preservation can never be taken away.

Task 1.1 (continued)

Question 4

Yes, Hobbes is a rationalist since he assumes that all individuals will see for themselves the self-destructive character of the state of nature and agree to form a society and a state. God, the maker of individuals, has ensured that all individuals are rational and can follow their self-interests. Hobbes believed that the logic of his argument would be irresistible to the people.

Hobbes tells us in *Leviathan* that everyone seeks to govern his or her own life. Again, note that this is essentially a liberal postulate. The role of the state is therefore to do collectively what individuals cannot do on their own.

Question 5

Hobbes sees nature as making all individuals free and equal. His notion of nature is in striking contrast to that of the ancient and medieval thinkers who saw nature as something that divided people and justified the state. For Hobbes, the state is not natural.

He believed that humans are by nature proud, egoistical and competitive. That is how they are made and nothing can change this. Although the state is not natural, egoism, pride and competition are. But this individualism is only negative when people see themselves only as individuals and ignore the need for collective agreement. Once they form contracts, they have to trust one another, and the state is a super contract in which individuals guarantee their survival by (as it were) collectivising their egoism. This is a modern view of nature, and many still find it compelling.

Task 1.2

Using this chapter and other resources available to you, answer the following questions:

1 Do you agree with the argument that 'neoliberalism' is too authoritarian and elitist to be called liberal?
2 Is 'social liberalism' really socialism rather than liberalism?
3 Must the concept of equality feature as part of liberalism?
4 'Classical liberalism is the true liberalism'. Discuss.
5 Is the notion of 'contract' essential to liberalism?

Guidance

Question 1

It is often argued that the neoliberalism of politicians like Thatcher and thinkers like Hayek represents a return to classical liberalism. Certainly Thatcher describes Hobbes

Task 1.2 (continued)

as her favourite philosopher, and many neoliberals have based their theories on thinkers like Locke. So it needs to be conceded that neoliberalism contains elements of classical liberalism. The free market, a limited state and the importance of consent are all liberal ideas that have been incorporated into neoliberal theory.

But liberalism does not regard individuals simply as free: it also regards them as equal. Every individual is in this sense the same. Historically liberalism arose out of Protestantism — a creed that ostensibly allows all individuals direct access to their creator. Neoliberalism regards people as free but it does not see them as equal, since it fears that equality will be interpreted in a socialist manner and used to interfere with the free market. Hence it is inclined to identify individuality with those who succeed in the market place, and in extreme circumstances allows the successful to rule over those who have failed until the conditions for a free society have been established. This is why both Thatcher and Hayek were admirers of the Chilean dictator, General Augusto Pinochet (1915–), because they felt he was using authoritarian power to establish a free society in which the market and competition could once again come into their own.

Question 2

From the middle of the nineteenth century onwards, liberals were confronted with social problems that early liberals had neither envisaged nor encountered. The Industrial Revolution meant that large numbers of people moved to cities and worked in factories. Urbanisation brought with it enormous problems. The invisible hand that was supposed to painlessly harmonise individual and social interests was not working in the way it had earlier. The poor were not only more numerous, but newly concentrated in cities and factories and beginning to demand social, economic and political rights. Collective organisations like trade unions and cooperatives were formed.

This provided liberals with a tremendous challenge. They had already abandoned the idea that all individuals had 'natural rights'. Now they went further. Individuality was not something everyone had: it was acquired socially, and unless there was reform — in health and safety in factories, in the recognition of trade unions and workers' rights — then the market itself would be discredited and revolutionary doctrines would win popular support. The social or new liberals took the view that socialism itself could be supported, if by socialism one meant social reforms that make individualism and the market viable and attractive. They were not socialists in the sense that they wanted a new system of society, but they did want reform and state intervention to ensure that life under a free enterprise system was tolerable and rewarding for the mass of the population.

Task 1.2 (continued)

Question 3

Being an individual is a necessary part of liberalism, but it is not enough. Because everyone is an individual, they are, in this respect, equal to everyone else. The right to be unequal, which Thatcher spoke of, is a problematic concept for liberalism, since this might suggest that not everyone is an individual, or that some are more individual than others.

Equality does not mean that everyone has the same resources, abilities or needs. But it does imply that, when it comes to the law, all are recognised as equals, and it is only because equality is seen as something 'substantive' that liberals have become nervous and wondered whether people really are the 'same'. But without some notion of equality, individuality is at risk. Liberalism is a universal doctrine, and unless all are individuals, no one can be an individual. Liberalism arises in conditions in which a privileged few have rights that are denied to others; once a doctrine denies that all are equal in some respect, it cannot be called liberal.

Question 4

'Classical liberalism' refers to the liberalism of the seventeenth and eighteenth centuries, when liberals believed that humans could be pictured in a state of nature, entering into society and forming a state through a social contract. This can be regarded as 'classical' because it reveals liberal ideas in their purest form. Individuals in the state of nature are isolated and self-contained. They are governed only by their own will and can do as they please. This state of nature might be self-destructive, as Hobbes envisaged, or relatively agreeable, as Locke theorised. Individuals might be rational egoists, consciously pursuing self-interest, or, as Rousseau argued, they are animal-like but distinguished from other natural creatures by their free will.

Once the notion of the state of nature is abandoned, then liberals admit elements of conservatism and socialism into their doctrine and it becomes less pure. On the other hand, to say that classical liberalism is the true liberalism is to ignore the history of political thought since the eighteenth century. Liberalism has had to change in order to survive, and the notion of a state of nature composed of isolated in dividuals is so fanciful that liberalism would not have been plausible if it had not recognised both the role society plays in creating individuality and the human capacity to reason. Contemporary liberals still take the view that the individual is more important than society and that the market and private property are essential to freedom, even though they differ radically from classical liberals on the degree of state and social intervention necessary to make it possible to see people as individuals.

Task 1.2 (continued)

Question 5

A contract is a device in which different people establish equal rights and duties. Contracts make people the same in the sense that each recognises their obligations to the other. Hence the early liberals believed that, to argue for the right of individuals to consent to their rulers and obligations to others, the formation of society and the state was a contract. This notion was abandoned in the late eighteenth century, but the idea of freedom being linked to, and arising out of, contract continues.

What attracts liberals to the mechanism of the market is that exchange can only be deemed fair when people are in some sense equal to one another. Critics argue that the device of contract conceals differences of power and resources, and new liberals have taken these criticisms on board by seeking to make contracts more transparent, so that those engaged can be more aware of their partner's real standing. Contract as an equalising device is central to liberalism, and it is impossible to think of any theory of emancipation that does not have reference to the idea of contract.

Useful websites

- www.en.wikipedia.org/wiki/Liberalism

Further reading

- Gray, J. (1995) *Liberalism*, Open University Press.
- Hobbes, T. *Leviathan*.
- Locke, J. *Two Treatises of Civil Government*.
- Mill, J. S. *On Liberty*.
- Rousseau, J.-J. *The Social Contract*.

How does liberalism view freedom and equality?

It is revealing that Hayek argues in *Constitution of Liberty* (1960) that equality means equality before the law, and not any kind of material equality. All liberals link freedom with equality, since it is impossible to regard people as individuals unless they have something in common. Freedom and equality denotes this similarity. These notions are central to liberalism, and although I want to argue that they are often interpreted in a problematic way, it is crucial to stress their importance and centrality.

Freedom and equality make liberalism a universal doctrine in the sense that all humans everywhere are deemed capable of exercising freedom. This is in contrast to ancient and medieval doctrines, as well as modern doctrines of the extreme right, such as fascism.

Free market liberalism: the classical roots

The problem with the liberal view of freedom and equality is that the market is taken for granted. In his work *The Political Theory of Possessive Individualism* (1962), C. B. Macpherson argues that Hobbes and Locke cannot be understood without a historical approach that emphasises the centrality of the market in their theories. Hobbes assumes that people are naturally competitive and self-interested, and this possessive individualism, as Macpherson calls it, stems from a belief that market relationships are themselves built into human nature. The war of all against all is a free market society without the state.

Locke's assumptions about the market are even more dramatic and explicit. Although his state of nature assumes that initially people should only appropriate what they can use, the invention of money enables them to accumulate wealth that goes far beyond what they need. People, Locke argues, consent to the role of money even while outside the social contract, and he takes for granted that part of an individual's labour is 'the turfs my servant has cut' — in other words, the labour of servants counts as the labour of those who employ them. From premises of freedom and equality, Locke ends up with a different view of consent and power to Hobbes, the most important end of the state being the protection of property. Locke makes it clear that the 'inconveniences' that necessitate the formation of society and the state are linked to the development of class divisions.

John Locke

Utilitarian and new liberal assumptions

Even when liberals have rejected the notion of a state of nature, they still continue to assume that freedom and equality are interpreted in the light of the assumption that market relations are natural. Adam Smith's famous comment in *The Wealth of Nations* (1776), where he argues that individuals naturally exchange things with one another, bears this point out. James Mill and Jeremy Bentham may have rejected the notion of natural rights, but the pursuit of utility is rooted in the view that individuals seek pleasure and avoid pain through market relations. For Bentham, the incentive to produce arises from the desire to avoid starvation and to enjoy the pleasure of abundance, and James Mill sees the market as providing an extractive power that enables us to render the person and properties of human beings subservient to our pleasures. To be free and equal is to act according to the dictates of the market.

Although the new liberals are critical of the market, in that they advocated welfare measures to offer workers a measure of social security, they still consider the market itself indispensable to freedom. As Anthony Arblaster rightly noted in *The Rise and Decline of Western Liberalism* (1984), the objective of the new liberals is not to abolish capitalism but rather to diffuse it among the community as a whole. They wish to make freedom and equality 'fairer' so that all can benefit from the market.

Freedom and equality in neoliberalism

It is often said that the rise of neoliberalism associated in particular with the UK Prime Minister Margaret Thatcher and the US President Ronald Reagan (1911–2004) involved a return to classical liberalism. But although there are similarities between the two, there is also a crucial difference. Despite their passionate support for freedom, neoliberals question equality as a value, and a classical liberal would never have spoken, as Thatcher did, of the 'right to be unequal'.

Of course, classical liberal thought only regards equal individuals as men with property, but for them equality is a guiding value linked to freedom. Classical liberals target the champions of medievalism and absolutism who argue for explicit repressive hierarchies, whereas neoliberals are reacting against socialists and social liberals who have extended classical liberal notions in a social direction. As noted above, the distinction between negative and positive liberty — freedom *from* and freedom *to* — is meaningless to classical liberalism, which takes for granted that individuals can do things and have power: the problem is having the space to exercise this capacity.

The particular position of Hayek

Hayek, who was knighted by Thatcher, makes it clear that freedom should be construed in militantly negative terms. Freedom should never be equated with power or capacity, since this would make it positive. He insists that equality cannot rest upon 'the factual equality of all men'. Equality can only mean equality before the law.

Indeed, some neoliberals are willing to support right-wing authoritarian regimes (both Thatcher and Hayek have expressed admiration

Friedrich von Hayek

for Chile's General Pinochet, who led a military coup against Allende's elected but radical left-wing government in 1973). Neoliberals like Hayek are reacting *against* social liberalism and socialism, and reject any values of the classical liberal tradition that might have provided an unwitting basis for left-wing ideas.

Keith Faulks has commented in *Citizenship in Modern Britain* (1998) that Hayek is really an elitist, and his version of liberalism is difficult to distinguish from authoritarian conservatism. Neoliberal policies have led to the creation of vast inequalities, and insofar as the modern USA approximates to a neoliberal utopia, it is a society that marginalises its inner-city areas and is afflicted by high rates of drug abuse and organised crime. The situation in New Orleans following the devastation of Hurricane Katrina has been likened to a Hobbesian state of nature — but a Hobbesian state of nature without the equality. Although the coexistence of the free market and a law-and-order state seems paradoxical, in fact, as Ian Gilmour (a Tory critic of the New Right) has remarked in his book *Dancing with Dogma* (1992), the establishment of a free market state is a 'dictatorial venture' which demands the submission of dissenting institutions and individuals.

The market and abstraction

All thinking involves abstraction. One can argue that our ideas always over-simplify the real world, and in that sense they are abstract. We could not think or speak without abstraction, since communication can only occur when the complexities of the real world are ordered and simplified. In this sense, abstraction is inevitable and positive.

But 'abstraction' also has a negative meaning, and to develop a critique of the liberal notion of freedom and equality it is crucial that this is clarified. Freedom and equality are interpreted as market exchanges, and when an exchange occurs, the exchangers have to find something that two (or more) different items have in common. Imagine a bartering situation in which a polished stick is exchanged for a bow and arrows. This is only possible because the people exchanging are able to 'abstract' something that equates the two different items they are exchanging. Money is even more 'abstract' since its purpose is simply to facilitate exchange.

Marx, who developed this argument in *Capital*, took the view that what makes it possible to exchange different objects is the labour that both embody, even though this labour is 'abstract'. It is not the labour that produced a particular object like a stick or a bow, but a generalised labour that both have in common. This is why he speaks of the 'metaphysical subtleties and theological niceties' of the exchange process. Some critics of the market, like C. B. Macpherson, see themselves as liberal democrats and oppose capitalism because they believe that it violates liberal principles. Instead of freedom and equality for all, society is divided into haves and have-nots.

Mystifying freedom and equality

However, we do not need to be wedded to a labour theory of value (as Marx was) to pursue a critique of abstraction. In my view, goods and services are the product of activity that goes well beyond labour as it is usually understood. This activity includes the unpaid work of a parent and the risk-taking of an investor. But the point remains. The exchange process is abstracted from the particular kinds of activity that produce things that are exchanged. But why is this a problem?

Take the Cape apple during the period of South African apartheid. As a piece of fruit, it fulfils a need, tastes good and may be relatively cheap. Open the apple any way you like, and you will not see the poverty and oppression, the discrimination and inhumanity inflicted upon those who produced it. This is because the market abstracts from the social relationships without which no object could be produced. The individuals who produce these goods are not seen as real people with real needs and particular identities. They are simply 'entities', each being the same as the other and all equally able to exercise 'choice'.

For Marx, this problem becomes even more acute when humans work for each other in a contractual way. When one sells one's services to an employer, the employee and employer are equated, even though the amount of social power that each commands is different. The contract that is formally or informally entered into does not register the differential facts about each party — that one partner to the contract may be, say, poor and female, the other male and prosperous. The two contractual partners are equal in a way that *abstracts* from the particular circumstances that make them what they are.

To return to the example of the Cape apple in the apartheid period: who would know from the apple itself that the workers producing them were paid not in cash, but in wine so that they became chronic alcoholics?

Making freedom and equality concrete: the problem of the environment

Emancipatory movements seek to make visible the conditions that the market renders abstract. They ask for the kind of concrete information that the exchange process conceals — the age, sex, wages, safety, health etc. of those whose activity

brings the object exchanged to fruition. Thus, for example, feminism argues that women, just as men, are individuals, socialism is concerned about the plight of the poor — those individuals without property — and anti-racism about the position of ethnic minorities.

Adam Smith, in a celebrated comment, argued that it is not humanity but 'self-love' that motivates people. However, this approach does not address unintended consequences of the kind in which cars, aeroplanes, factories and so on lead to the destruction of the environment. It assumes that there is automatic harmony between the individual's self interest and the collective good. Environmentalists are right to insist that the freedom and equality of individuals can have extremely negative consequences. It is not surprising that champions of the free market are reluctant to admit the realities of, say, global warming, since the destruction of the environment is the product of an invisible hand that is supposed to lead to the wellbeing of all.

Again, ecological and environmental movements seek to render market relations more concrete and transparent, so that one can see the social and natural realities that result from exchanges. All solutions to these problems, from the most moderate to the most extreme, involve going beyond the market in the way that consequences are costed and analysed. When one looks concretely at the activity of free and equal individuals, a different picture results. Thus, air flights in the UK might be cheap as far as the market is concerned, but what if the notion of consumption is extended to take account of noise problems, congestion and the depletion of the ozone layer?

The market and freedom

Liberals have assumed that the market is indispensable to freedom, and Norman Barry, in his *Introduction to Modern Political Theory* (1981), sees the market as a mechanism that allows consent but no power. People who exchange goods and services can be said to exercise their will autonomously. It is true that to enter market relations a person has to exercise choice, but whether this is compatible with freedom depends upon how constraining the circumstances are under which such a choice is made. If the choice is between starvation and working for another, say, does this constitute an authentic choice? A woman may 'choose' to sell her body in order to survive, but what kind of choice is this?

C. B. Macpherson argues in his critical assessment of *Capitalism and Freedom* by Milton Friedman (1912–) that exchanges in a capitalist society cannot be said to be free and voluntary when workers lack sufficient capital to work for themselves. Choice surely implies meaningful alternatives, and a worker has no choice but to enter the labour market. In Macpherson's view, this constitutes 'coercion', not choice, and only when (in what he terms a simple market model) a household is able to produce sufficient goods and services to be self-reliant can it be said that the decision to enter the market is one of meaningful choice.

Freedom, coercion and determinism

Macpherson's arguments raise the question of determinism, because it can be argued that even in the simple market model circumstances still 'compel' a person to enter into exchange relations. Marx, for example, speaks of capitalists themselves being coerced by the laws of competition, and commodity producers being subject to what he calls 'the coercion exerted by the presence of their mutual interests'. It seems to me that it is problematic to speak of coercion in this context, since coercion implies, in my view, the threat of force, and neither capitalist commodity producers, nor indeed workers, are in this sense coerced into market relations.

Marx speaks of humans entering into relations of production 'independent of their will'. But does this suggest that people have no freedom and are mere automatons that are forced to produce? It is clear that no one can produce unless they choose to do so, but his argument is that humans cannot survive unless production takes place. In this sense, people enter into relations of production 'independent of their will' since the most parasitic of individuals cannot live if no one is producing any wealth.

The real question is not whether the market constrains — since this is true of all circumstances — but whether it constrains in a way in which human development is advanced or retarded. Freedom has been defined as the 'recognition of necessity'. We can certainly change things when we act, but we always act in a particular context and situation.

The problem with the market is that it is liable to conceal circumstances, so that the exchange process appears to rely merely upon the will of participants, and not upon resources, personality and the conditions in which each works. It is impossible to analyse freedom and equality meaningfully unless one takes account of these determining circumstances. Hence I would argue that people who 'choose' to sell their bodies as prostitutes are invariably responding to circumstances of a dire and inhuman kind. The more that exchange relations become transparent, the more that choice can be said to be genuine. Making freedom and equality concrete means accepting that people are individuals with

choice, but also looking at what they do and who they are in a way that takes account of the circumstances moulding them.

A fair and just process of exchange

Source: *Social Studies Review*, Vol. 1, No. 2, p. 32.

Figure 1.1 Marx's view of the fetishistic appearance of the capitalist system

The exploitative character of capitalist production

Source: *Social Studies Review*, Vol. 1, No. 2, p. 32.

Figure 1.2 Marx's view of the social reality of the capitalist system

Conclusion

The problem with liberalism is that its principles are abstract, by which we mean that they ignore the social realities of the formally equal partners to a contract. This abstraction mars the liberal analysis of freedom and equality. People are seen as property — each individual has property over himself. Although liberals from the end of the eighteenth century had generally rejected the notion of natural rights and argued that humans were naturally social beings, they still saw individuals as 'atoms' that took decisions in isolation from one another. It is true that individual drive and initiative are among the factors that mould us, but they are not the sole factors. Aspects of our social and natural environment also play their part.

Liberalism assumes that the relations between humans and nature (i.e. *human nature*) take the form of an exchange between individuals through the market.

This exchange ignores the particular facts of each person's context (whether they are rich or poor, men or women etc.), and makes it appear that the parties to the exchange are the 'same'. Until the twentieth century, liberals regarded individuals as men rather than women, since individuals were rational property owners, and women were seen as neither. Although property was supposedly produced by labour, in practice liberals allowed some to work for others. Whole countries could be owned as the property of those who made 'profitable' use of them, so that liberals until relatively recently supported colonialism and imperialism.

Making freedom and equality concrete involves making the wider costs and consequences of exchanges known to the participants, so that relationships become more developmental and thus humane.

Summary

- Classical liberals like Hobbes and Locke present individuals as free and equal, but this freedom and equality arises in a state of nature in which there are no social relationships between people. They take it for granted that the market is natural, and that freedom and equality arise out of market exchanges.
- This view of the market persists even when liberals reject the concept of a state of nature and the idea of the state as the product of a social contract. Utilitarians assume that individuals pursue pleasure and avoid pain in market-type exchanges with one another. New liberals are critical of the free market, but in arguing the case for state regulation and intervention they assume that freedom and equality are fairer, because they enable the market to work in everyone's interests.
- Neoliberals claim to be returning to the classical liberal tradition. In reality they are reacting to the interventions sanctioned by new liberalism, and they defend freedom as 'the right to be unequal' (something that no classical liberal would have ever said). Hayek insists freedom is so negative that a person can be free to starve, since freedom is not about power and capacity, but the right not to be interfered with by the state and bullying individuals.
- The problem with the liberal analysis of freedom and equality is that it is abstract. This means that it ignores the specific circumstances in which particular individuals act, and in this way betrays its roots in the market.
- Freedom and equality are valuable assumptions but they need to be looked at concretely. This can only be done when full account is taken of the circumstances in which individuals act and choose, since these circumstances make individuals what they are. Individuals can change these circumstances, but to do so they must recognise the impact they make as accurately and comprehensively as possible.

Task 2.1

Read the passage below and answer the questions that follow.

Thatcherism and liberalism

Thatcher was often accused of being a Whig, or an old-fashioned liberal, by her critics. There is certainly something in this critique. As prime minister she showed that she was a passionate free marketeer and did not hesitate to knight Hayek, although Hayek makes it clear in his *Constitution of Liberty* that he is not a conservative. Thatcher pays tribute to Hayek in *The Downing Street Years* (1993), where she says that his book *Road to Serfdom* left 'a permanent mark on my political character, making me a long-term optimist for free enterprise.'

Margaret Thatcher

Keith Faulks has seen her as a champion of the New Right, arguing that her view that people fail because they are unworthy carries 'to its logical conclusion the abstract and elitist logic of the individualism in neoliberal political theory'.

Thatcher sold off council houses, preferred private transport and expressed scepticism about the existence of society as a force that stands over the individual. She championed the interests of the 'citizen' against established institutions like the civil service. She argued for an abstract view of freedom. Her radicalism seemed 'un-Tory' in character, and she regarded traditional conservatism as far too willing to accept what she considered to be a 'socialist consensus'.

On the other hand, it is easy to exaggerate her apparent break from conservatism. The Falklands War showed that she had traditional conservative sympathies for the 'kith and kin' in the colonies; she was strongly opposed to national liberation movements like the African National Congress; she appointed hereditary peers to the House of Lords; and, although a woman, was unimpressed by feminist arguments. Her opposition to the European Union drew upon an English nationalism that also manifested itself in 'concern' about immigration and multiculturalism. She subscribed to the view that leaders must lead, and that inequality in society was natural and should be accepted.

It is useful to draw up a list of Thatcher's liberal characteristics and conservative characteristics to see whether on balance she really was a liberal or a Tory at heart.

Task 2.1 (continued)

Questions

1 'Thatcher's passionate belief in freedom makes her a liberal.' Discuss.

2 What was Thatcher's attitude towards equality?

3 Was Thatcher a nationalist?

4 Was Thatcher's attitude to the European Union liberal?

5 Do you think that on balance, Thatcher was as much a Tory as she was a liberal?

Guidance

Question 1

It is certainly true that Thatcher was a passionate advocate of freedom, and she saw freedom in traditionally liberal terms as freedom of the market. She argued strongly for choice; policies such as selling off council houses to tenants and lowering the tax rate were linked to this notion. So was the fact that, under her administration, growing numbers of people bought their own cars and private transport substantially increased.

But does this make her a liberal? There are two points here. First, she was not a new or social liberal. Many of her policies led to a weakening of the welfare state — the achievement of new liberals like David Lloyd George and William Beveridge — and it could be argued that Thatcherism involved dismantling many aspects of the postwar settlement. The second point raises the question of whether she was a classical liberal. Hayek was knighted and Thatcher feted his work, but he and others are really *neo*liberals rather than classical liberals. The idea that you can be 'free to starve' is not a classical liberal dictum, and the notion that freedom is simply negative — freedom from and not freedom to — is neoliberal rather than classical liberal.

Question 2

Thatcher took the view that people have the right to be unequal. Strictly speaking, she accepted that everyone is equal under the law, but went along with Hayek's argument that this is not a 'factual' equality. Under her administration there was a proliferation of homeless people, with the gap between the rich and the poor increasing.

Thatcher identified the notion of equality with socialism, and felt that egalitarian policies undermined the entrepreneurial spirit of the free market. She passionately championed the individual, but her critics argued that she concentrated upon individuals who had benefited from the market, and pushed to one side those who lost out. She felt that a commitment to equality was linked to interference with freedom and would inevitably be used to justify high taxation and an extension of state power. Although the coercive powers of the state increased during her period of office, its welfare functions were cut back. Benefits were reduced, and those who were 'failures' were seen as passive rather than active citizens.

Task 2.1 (continued)

Question 3

Thatcher took the view that people belong to particular nations and this plays a key role in forging their identity. She had a static and traditionalist view of nationhood and tended to identify the British with the English. For that reason she supported the Conservative Party's traditional opposition to devolution, seeing it as an unnecessary and potentially dangerous concession to minority nationalisms.

Was Thatcher a British nationalist? She was not particularly concerned about the position of ethnic minorities, and although she clearly rejected the racism of the extreme right, she regarded immigrants as valuable for their economic rather than cultural contribution. During the Falklands War she was fiercely pro-British, and critics have argued that she did not see Argentineans as entitled to the same rights as the British. She was sceptical about cosmopolitanism, regarding it as a fuzzy idealism, and during her administration the notion of the supremacy of the English and English speakers was stressed.

Question 4

Thatcher was in favour of the European Union (EU) as a 'common market'. She supported the UK joining an economic union because this was good for business and investment. But culturally and politically she had grave reservations.

Thatcher was convinced that people see themselves as members of a nation state. She feared that the EU was becoming a super state, expanding its political controls over the governments of its member states and moving towards a federal organisation in which the UK would simply be one of its local units. For these reasons she was a Eurosceptic rather than a liberal, and her famous attacks on 'Brussels' demonstrated a belief in Victorian nationalism that her critics felt was out of touch with modern realities. She negotiated a budget rebate with the EU authorities because she was convinced that the UK was paying too much to European finances.

Linked to her traditional view of the English and the nation state was her scepticism towards those nationalisms she regarded as antithetical to the UK's interests, for example Irish nationalism. She took a strong line with Irish Republican hunger strikers, and was unsympathetic to the call by the African National Congress of South Africa for sanctions to isolate the apartheid system.

Question 5

Thatcher made Victorian versions of liberalism respectable. Take her celebrated comment that 'there is no such thing as society'. Although she insisted that she recognised the existence of families and groups, this kind of comment is reminiscent of nineteenth-century utilitarian statements. Her hostility to the civil service and the

Task 2.1 (continued)

establishment indicated a liberal belief in the 'small man' — an individual who stands out against the collective.

On the other hand, many of her policies have roots in Toryism rather than in liberalism. Her nationalism and identification of the English with the British are described above. She was a strong patriot, and although she is supposed to have fallen out with the Queen, she had a powerful respect for tradition and appointed hereditary peers to the Lords at a time when reform of that institution was in the air. She was not sympathetic to feminism, and took the view — in her dealings with the Soviet Union, for example — that different people do different things in different parts of the world. She disliked the internationalist implications of traditional liberal theory.

What complicates this question is that in the nineteenth century liberalism and conservatism intertwined (think of the position of Burke, who can be described as a liberal Tory). Thatcher can therefore be described as a conservative liberal, provided we think of liberalism in Victorian rather than in social liberal terms.

Task 2.2

Using this chapter and other resources available to you, answer the following questions:

1 Do you agree with Adam Smith that it is part of human nature to 'truck and barter'?
2 Is it possible to be a liberal and a critic of the market?
3 Does the exchange process have to conceal the real identity of the partners to the transaction?
4 Can liberalism deal with the problem of the environment?
5 Why did the new liberals begin to advocate policies that make inroads into the market?

Guidance
Question 1
Smith and other members of the Scottish Enlightenment thought that the state of nature concept of classical liberalism was implausible. Smith took a position similar to Hume's in arguing that the idea of the state as a social contract should be rejected, but he did believe that market exchanges were natural to humans.

The notion of human nature arises out of our perception of the relationship of humans to nature. Although markets are old, they are not eternal. For many thousands of years humans lived in small communities that were mostly self-sufficient, and 'human nature' expressed itself in the norms appropriate for hunters and gatherers.

Task 2.2 (continued)

It is unwise to assume that behaviour in one historical period represents the way people 'are' — trucking and bartering are no more 'natural' than the concept of the individual as an isolated, self-contained being. Human nature does exist, because people cannot survive without producing and relating to one another. But how they produce and how they relate to one another is always changing, and liberals are wrong to imagine that institutions and norms that they hold precious will always exist.

Question 2

To most liberals, the answer must be a resounding no. The market is seen as an institutional bastion of freedom, so that to challenge the market is to challenge liberal values in general. But what about those who do badly as a result of the market? There is evidence that the market can divide society into haves and have-nots; that women do less well than men in market relationships; and that the less economically developed world enters into trading relationships that favour rich countries and makes them still richer.

If liberalism is concerned about the wellbeing of everyone and insists that all are free and equal, then it could be argued that the market undermines rather than advances liberal values. Emancipatory movements, like feminism and socialism, have their historic roots in liberalism, and new liberals argue that regulation and state control are necessary if liberal institutions are to continue to enjoy popular support. It is true that most new liberals support a humane version of capitalism and the market, but it is possible for radicals like C. B. Macpherson to take the view that liberalism implies a participatory democracy that the market and consumerism prevents. Such liberals would be better described as post-market theorists, since they are less concerned to reject the market than to gradually make exchanges transparent and fair, so that human need rather than an ability to pay becomes the determining criteria for the distribution of scarce goods.

Question 3

The market constitutes a great advance in the historical development of society. To exchange goods on a significant scale, something in common must be found in different entities. Given that in a simple barter situation a polished stick exchanges for a carved piece of stone, how do we decide that two different things can change places? As more and more goods are produced for a market, one commodity has to be set aside to act as the medium of exchange — money. Locke argues that the agreement to use gold and silver as media of exchange makes it possible to accumulate wealth and get round the problem of surplus goods spoiling. With the rise of capitalism, not only are goods exchanged, but one person sells his or her services to another and is paid a wage that is deemed an equivalent.

Task 2.2 (continued)

What makes the market historically significant is that ideas of freedom and equality arise from it that challenge older notions of people locked up in hierarchical roles. In a market-dominated society, those who participate in the exchange process are deemed equal. They contract with each other, and do not force one another to do things against their will. Hence the liberal notions of freedom and equality are linked to those of consent and toleration. But, as the new liberals and socialists discovered, the equation that occurs is a formal one. One party might be rich, the other poor; one a self-assured man, the other a vulnerable woman, and so on. Rousseau's search for an 'authentic' social contract highlights the point that the market process conceals the actual resources and real power that a party commands.

Is this inherent in the exchange process? Exchanges can be made far more transparent, so that the real identity of the people transacting becomes visible. But since the purpose of the exchange is to buy and sell goods and services, then some degree of concealment and 'abstraction' in the exchange process is inevitable.

Question 4

The classical liberal assumption is that the individual is the focus of attention, not a wider collectivity. In the state of nature, people are deemed to survive without society; even when liberals have abandoned this thesis, they still take the view that there is a natural harmony between the interests of the individual and society as a whole. This is the essence of Smith's invisible hand: people pursue self-interest and the 'whole' takes care of itself.

The new liberals became acutely aware of the way in which industry was polluting the environment, as well as having negative effects on the wellbeing of workers in factories. Regulation and a more positive role for the state are therefore the new watchwords of the social liberal tradition. Liberalism can deal with the environment, but to do so inroads have to be made into the market, as people pursuing their self-interests can damage rather than enhance wider social and natural habitats. The private car is classic example that illustrates this problem. People who buy and drive private vehicles cause asthma, congestion and the destruction of the ozone layer — even though they don't intend to.

This notion of unintended consequences compels us to look beyond the market and self-interest, and to work out a system of costing that takes account of problems that result when, for example, people take 'cheap' air flights abroad. Liberalism can deal with the problem of the environment, but to do so it has to take account of the social and global consequences of the exchange process, and move away from classical assumptions.

Task 2.2 (continued)

Question 5

The new liberals became increasingly aware that people owe far more to society than they may realise. From the late eighteenth century, liberals had abandoned the idea that humans exist as isolated, self-contained beings in a state of nature. But the implications of humans as *social* animals is not really digested by the utilitarians, for example, who still identify the idea of a collectivity with repression and autocracy.

The Industrial Revolution was a harsh teacher. In Britain, for example, not only did the Chartists demand that all males should have voting rights, but they insisted that the vote was not merely a political, but a 'knife and fork' (that is, an economic) question. It was becoming clear to liberals (and conservatives as well) that the free market on its own, as it were, would lead to increased social polarisation, and even revolution. Reform was essential if people were to have a stake in the community, and these reforms all make inroads into the market. A reappraisal of basic concepts took place. J.S. Mill is often thought of as a classical liberal because he is concerned about the right of individuals to act in ways that may displease others but does not harm their interests. But if you look at Mill's theory carefully, what do you find? A recognition that society can certainly intervene when an individual harms another's interest, and, even more than this, a belief that such intervention is permissible when individuals harm themselves, acting in ways that cannot be reversed.

New liberals recognised that the state might be a positive source of good and that individuals can be harmed and coerced by others, even when the latter do not intend to harm society. Talents and skills that earlier liberals had considered innate or God-given (such as the private property of fortunate individuals) were increasingly seen as being linked to social processes, so it is perfectly permissible for society to expect resources and support from the individual in return.

Useful websites

- www.en.wikipedia.org/wiki/Classical_liberalism

Further reading

- Arblaster, A. (1984) *The Rise and Decline of Western Liberalism*, Blackwell.
- Faulks, K. (1998) *Citizenship in Modern Britain*, Edinburgh University Press.
- Hayek, F. *Constitution of Liberty*.
- Macpherson, C. B. (1977) *The Life and Times of Liberal Democracy*, Oxford University Press.

How democratic
is liberalism?

Liberalism and democracy are often regarded as synonyms. But this does not only make democracy an extremely vague concept, it undermines our understanding of liberalism as well. It is wrong to assume that liberals automatically supported the case for democracy. In fact, it was only in the twentieth century that liberals felt inclined to champion the political rights of the poor and the working class.

Conservative misconceptions

T. D. Weldon, a linguistic analyst, argued in his classic work *The Vocabulary of Politics* (1953) that 'democracy', 'capitalism' and 'liberalism' are all alternative names for the same thing. But this view ignores the historical development of these concepts. Historically liberals were not democrats, even if they were attacked as democrats by conservative critics of liberalism.

Locke, for example, took it for granted that those who could vote were men, merchants and landowners, and the question of universal suffrage (even for men only) is not even raised in his *Two Treatises of Government* (1689). Liberals declared that men were free and equal, and although this was taken by conservatives to denote support for democracy, it was not so.

A hapless King Charles I (he reigned from 1625–49) reproached English parliamentarians who had taken him prisoner for 'labouring to bring about democracy'. Yet it is clear that their leader, Oliver Cromwell (who ruled from 1653–58), and his puritan gentry did not believe in democracy. Even the left wing of the movement — the Levellers — wished to exclude 'servants' and 'paupers' from the franchise. Cromwellians were alarmed that the egalitarian premises of liberal theory might extend the freedom to rule to smaller property owners.

Early US attitudes

It is important to note that the US Constitution was formulated in 1787 by people who were more than a little reluctant to describe themselves as democrats. Throughout the secret discussions at the Constitutional Convention, great distrust was expressed towards 'the common man and democratic rule'. The struggles that had ensued in the 11 years since the Declaration of Independence appeared to many to exemplify 'the turbulence and follies of democracy'.

In his essay 'Federalist No. 10', James Madison (1751–1836), one of the founders of the US Constitution, described democracies as 'incompatible with personal security or the rights of property'. Under a democracy, he argued, an egalitarian factionalism is likely to generate 'a rage of paper money, for an abolition of debts or for some other improper or wicked project'. John Jay (1745–1829), one of the authors of the *Federalist Papers*, declared that the 'people who own the country should govern it'. All the Federalists endorsed the view that popular government becomes extremely dangerous when measures are decided by a strong and 'overbearing' majority. These reservations are not difficult to understand when we remember that the Federalists regarded themselves as liberal republicans, not democrats.

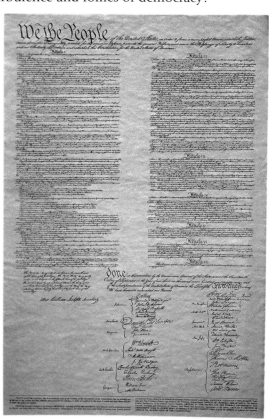

The entire original US Constitution, showing the signatures at the end

Jefferson: a great democrat?

All this raises a challenging question. If the US Constitution was founded by people who were (to put it mildly) unenthusiastic about popular rule, why should Alexis de Tocqueville (1805–59) and his admirers regard the USA as the classic home of liberal democracy? It might be argued that the Founding Fathers were conservatively minded republicans who lost influence to the radically minded republican democrats who came to dominate the political scene after 1800, and that most Americans identified less with Madison than with Thom as Jefferson (1743–1826). Jefferson, the author of the Declaration of Independence (1787), is described by Tocqueville as 'the greatest democrat ever to spring from American democracy'.

The problem is that Jefferson not only admired the *Federalist Papers*, but shared to the full what Louis Hartz in *The Liberal Tradition in America* (1955) has called 'America's neurotic terror of the majority'. His democratic credentials are hardly above dispute. He favoured constitutional checks and balances as a way of preventing what he called 'elective despotism'. He was not enthusiastic about (male) universal suffrage, and he took the view that voters should be male farmers who owned property. In other words, Jefferson, whose very name seems synonymous with democracy, was really a liberal and a republican in his way of thinking.

Tension and harmony in troubled relationship

The US political scientist Richard Hofstadter has commented on how modern US folklore anachronistically assumes that liberalism and democracy are identical, and that it misses the point Bernard Crick makes in his work, *In Defence of Politics*, that there is 'tension as well as harmony' between the two concepts. There is *tension* because liberals did not intend universal rights to apply to all adults; and *harmony* because their critics from the right assumed that they did, and their critics from the left felt that if rights were universal in theory, then they should be universal in practice. In other words, without liberalism it is impossible to have democracy.

Do not assume that liberal theorists were necessarily democratic in orientation. The Founding Fathers wanted space for some popular pressure, so that if the poor could not plunder the rich, then neither could the rich plunder the poor. A delegate called George Mason told the Constitutional Convention that while in the past 'we had been too democratic', he was afraid that 'we should incautiously run to the opposite extreme'. The people must have a voice in making the laws, since, as John Adams (1735–1826) put it, there can be no free government 'without a democratical branch in the Constitution'.

This is the point. Democracy was to be one element within a mixed or balanced Constitution designed to promote the interests and rights of every class in the machinery of government. But if the Founding Fathers were basically liberals who took the view that democracy was incompatible with the rights of property, how was a compromise solution to be viable?

The rights of property

Rousseau (contrary to what is often said) felt that democracy was unworkable. As he put it in *The Social Contract*, democracy assumed a perfectionism that human nature belied, and was a form of government ever liable to 'civil wars and intense agitations'. The social state, he argued, is only advantageous when all have something, and no one has too much.

The Founding Fathers in the USA were liberals rather than democrats in a society in which there was a uniquely wide spread of property ownership. If US liberals were willing to contemplate a popular element in their Constitution, this was because the 'poor' themselves owned property and hence could more or less be relied upon to act as 'responsible citizens' with a stake in society.

This is the point to which Tocqueville returns over and over again. Most people who are rich begin by being poor: in the nineteenth century there was greater equality of wealth and 'mental endowments' in the USA than in any other country or in any age of recorded history. It is not just that the poor in the USA might have seemed rich when compared to the poor of Europe. It is that they owned their wealth as individual landowners.

Tocqueville's analysis

According to Tocqueville's analysis, the USA is seen as democratic because there are no proletarians, although it should be noted that there *were* dispossessed Indians and enslaved black people, whose plunder and exploitation was hardly incidental to the property ownership of most white people. For Tocqueville, the secret of the USA's success is that 'everyone' has property to defend. Hence the extraordinary paradox. The USA is the land of democracy *par excellence,* and yet in no other country in the world is there a greater love of property. Maxims called democratic in France would be outlawed in the USA.

Tocqueville's analysis of the 1830s captures the liberal egalitarianism of what has been called 'Jacksonian democracy' (after President Andrew Jackson) — a democracy based upon a sense of common identity derived from fighting Indians, enslaving black people and owning land. Hofstadter describes this as the 'philosophy of a rising middle class', and it was this philosophy that informed the liberalism of President Lincoln too. Lincoln attacked slavery not because he was opposed to racism, but because he feared that the spread of slavery would undermine the status of free white labour. And what made labour free? The fact that the hired labourer of today can hire labour tomorrow. If this position is egalitarian, the equality it champions is the equality of property owners in what is still basically a pre-industrial age.

The disappearance of equality

Yet it was clear to Tocqueville that equality in the USA had a curiously illusory quality to it. In the first place, as he notes, democratic institutions (as Tocqueville regarded them) arouse a passion for equality that they are not really able to satisfy. Just as people think that they have equality within their grasp, it slips elusively through their fingers. Second, and even more seriously, a 'natural impulse' (as Tocqueville calls it) is 'throwing up an aristocracy out of the bosom of democracy'.

In a chapter that is almost Marxian in tone, Tocqueville argues that as conditions become more equal, the need for manufactured products extends. The rich open establishments with a strict division of labour, and the effect of this is to make workers degraded and dependent. The employer becomes more like the 'administrator of a huge empire' and the employee 'more like a brute': 'each occupies a place made for him, from which he does not move'. This is a development that causes anxiety for the 'friend of democracy', but there are two factors that give Tocqueville cause for comfort.

The first is that the development of this manufacturing aristocracy only flourishes in some industrial sectors — 'an exception, a monstrosity, within the general social condition', which still tends towards equality of conditions and rising wages. Second, while he argues that this manufacturing aristocracy is 'one of the hardest that has ever appeared on earth', it is also one of the 'most restrained and least dangerous'. The manufacturing aristocracy lack the cohesion, corporate spirit and community of interest to become a ruling class, since they seem too busy competing among themselves to exercise any collective control over the state.

Yet on both these arguments Tocqueville was vulnerable. John Stuart Mill wondered, in his review of Tocqueville's *Democracy in America*, just how 'exceptional' manufacturing aristocracies were going to remain, given the British experience's suggestion that in all industrial 'callings' prosperity brings less rather than more equality. Great fortunes are continually accumulated but seldom distributed.

Mill's point was a salient one. The US census of 1870 showed that the trading classes were growing far more quickly than the population as a whole. By 1873 the USA had experienced its first industrial depression — a development spawning bankruptcies, mergers, wage cutting, urban riots, nationwide strikes and the use of troops by business-minded governments. With industrialisation helping to speed up the concentration of wealth and power, 'the New World was beginning,' as E. F. Goldman puts it in *Rendezvous with Destiny* (1955), 'to repeat the Old World's dismal story'.

The robber barons

The 'Gilded Age', the age of the robber baron, had arrived. Robber barons were the industrial giants who dominated US society after the civil war. It was becoming clear, as the reform movements of the day protested, that the rich were making an impact on the political process in the precisely the way Tocqueville had said couldn't happen. Bribing congressmen and buying legislatures were seen as integral parts of the capitalist ethic. The Senate became known as 'the Millionaires' Club' and reformers targeted what they called (as Goldman notes) 'the alliance between industrialists and the political class which thinks like the industrialists'. Manufacturing aristocrats, for all their internal competition, were coalescing into a new ruling class.

But what did this mean for the concept of liberalism and its relation to democracy? The Industrial Revolution, coming in the wake of the civil war, raised the problem of continuity with the past. Andrew Carnegie symbolised the expansiveness and optimism of the new era, and what is significant about his *Triumphant Capitalism* (1886) is that it inaugurated a new way of looking at democracy.

The traditional argument had been that democracy was simply one element — the popular element — to be checked and balanced by others in the Constitution. Now, according to Carnegie's argument, democracy stood for the 'whole' Constitution. Writers noted the plutocratic element within American democracy (i.e. the rule of the wealthy) but saw this plutocracy as democracy in its true form. Anyone who challenged this manufacturing aristocracy challenged democracy — the village storekeeper and the Standard Oil company enter the arena on equal terms — and the tension between democracy and liberalism vanished into thin air.

The traditional voice

Under the impact of the First World War pressures for a *rapprochement* between liberalism and democracy became evident in other countries as well. In the UK, no one, Crick argues, would have described the government as a democracy in 1913, and yet, one year later, the country went to war in order, it was said, to preserve this (if somewhat flexible) notion. Extirpation of the Bolshevik menace was presented in the name of democracy. The tension between liberalism still occasionally appeared; a 1920s government publication in the USA described democracy as 'a government of the masses…Attitude towards property is communistic — negating property rights…results in demagogism, license, agitation, discontent, anarchy.' Thus spoke the voice of traditional liberalism!

The argument of C. B. Macpherson

Macpherson argued in *The Life and Times of Liberal Democracy* (1977) that, in the seventeenth century, nobody who was anybody would have said they were a democrat. As far as people of substance — landowners, clergy, merchants and lawyers — were concerned, liberalism might be acceptable but democracy was a term of abuse: a system of government fatal to the individual and all the graces of civilised government.

Macpherson is particularly interested in how and why liberals became democrats. Democratic visions have, he argues, recurred continually for over 2000 years, and he contrasts what he calls the 'one-class model' of the ancient world (also endorsed by Rousseau and Jefferson), with later 'class-divided models' of liberal democracy.

This characterisation is confusing for two reasons. The first is that there were class divisions in the so-called one class model, since in ancient Greece democracy was the rule of poor men, who ruled over women, aliens and slaves. Neither Rousseau nor Jefferson supported the case for universal suffrage, and they would have excluded the poor, dependents and women from voting. Because they supported a society of independent property owners, they were liberals rather than democrats.

The second problem with Macpherson's argument is that if 'one-class democrats' did not embrace the whole community, should we call them democrats at all? Rousseau condemned slavery as contrary to nature, and yet he wondered whether there are not some situations (like ancient Greece) in which 'the citizen can be perfectly free only when the slave is most a slave'. Jefferson obviously had little sympathy for the 'merciless Indian savages', the term used in the *Declaration of Independence* for the Native Americans robbed of their land.

The 'conversion' of Bentham and James Mill

Democracy was not an issue until the late eighteenth century. It only became an issue when those excluded from political power began to demand their rights. In terms of British political theory, the apparent conversion of liberals to democrats starts with Bentham and James Mill.

The support of these two for universal suffrage was only grudging and cautious. Bentham initially favoured a limited franchise that would exclude the

poor, the uneducated and women. But in a Europe radicalised by the French Revolution, some British liberals became conscious of the need to cultivate popular support if the old Whig oligarchy of landed and financial interests was to be displaced. In 1820 Bentham declared that while he would happily settle for a limited householder franchise, this would not satisfy those excluded — who perhaps constituted 'a majority of male adults'.

James Mill's 'conversion' was similarly cautious. In his *Essay on Government* (1820) he asserts that people need a vote to protect their interests, and yet he proceeds to argue that these interests could be protected even if all women, all men under 40, and the poorest third of the male population over 40 were excluded from the vote. Macpherson describes James Mill as 'less than a whole-hearted democrat', but what Mill and Bentham's analysis revealed is this question: if a liberal is to become a democrat, is espousing universal suffrage enough?

Natural rights and property

Liberals in the nineteenth century became nervous that the natural rights tradition might be used against property (as had been the case in the latter phases of the French Revolution). 'Utility' seems a much safer and more respectable way of defending liberty than the notion of natural rights, since class divisions could no longer be ignored. The idea that everyone had the same innate rights no longer seemed plausible.

Bentham himself notes that the great mass of citizens live at a basic subsistence level, having no other resource than their industry, and that given this division the famous happiness principle runs into difficulty. The incentive to produce is supposed to arise from a desire to avoid the pain of starvation, and to enjoy the pleasure of acquiring abundance. But if property owners are cushioned by their wealth against the fear of starvation, and workers cannot obtain abundance no matter how hard they work, then there are two orders of individuals. One enjoys the pleasure, the other suffers the pain, and the universal generalisation no longer holds.

Jeremy Bentham

The notion of equality therefore becomes increasingly troublesome. According to Macpherson, Bentham insists that when security of property comes into conflict with equality, it is equality that 'yields'. Abundance for the few means subsistence for the many. In theory, it is happiness that is maximised; in practice, it is wealth. But if society is deeply divided, will not universal suffrage expose the property owner to a 'tyranny of majority' by those who are poor?

Bentham only accepted the case for universal suffrage when he was convinced that the poor would not use their votes to destroy private property. James Mill was even more forthright. He argued that, on acquiring the vote, workers would still continue to regard the middle class as the class that gives science, art and legislation 'their most distinguished ornaments' and as the chief source of all that is 'refined and exalted in human nature'. The business of government remains the business of the rich.

Is there a conflict between protecting property and extending suffrage? Some liberals continued to believe this to be the case. Thomas Babington Macaulay (1800–59) declared that the democracy of the kind 'Mr Mill' proposed would create a situation in which (as he rather extravagantly puts it) 'the rich would be as unmercifully pillaged as under a Turkish pasha'. Mill and Bentham saw the USA as a society in which relatively poor people behaved 'responsibly', but Macaulay was quick to point out that conditions there were exceptional and could quickly change. Macpherson describes Mill and Bentham's model as one of 'protective democracy', of which it could be asked that although political rights are given to the poor, do the poor have power?

The position of John Stuart Mill

This question led John Stuart Mill to adopt a curiously contradictory response to the liberal arguments of his father and Bentham. On the one hand, as is noted in Chapter 1, he embraces a less mechanistic notion of the individual, arguing that the pursuit of pleasure must be understood in 'the largest sense' since people are progressive beings. In *On Liberty* he speaks of human nature as a tree that 'requires to grow and develop itself on all sides'. He refers sympathetically to the plight of workers and argues for the empowerment of women, leading Macpherson to argue that Mill moved from a protective to a developmental view of democracy.

On the other hand, Mill began to doubt whether his father was right in assuming that workers would necessarily accept middle-class leadership. Given the support of workers for Chartism — a radical political doctrine of the 1840s — Mill wonders in his *Autobiography* whether Macaulay did not have a serious

point and that it was wrong to assume 'an identity of interest between the governing body and the community at large' as a result of a mere election. He wrote that he had come to dread 'the ignorance and especially the selfishness and brutality of the mass'.

Democracy vs socialism

In his *Considerations of Representative Government* John Stuart Mill advocates the exclusion from the franchise of paupers, bankrupts, illiterates and non-taxpayers, and argues the case for a system of plural voting in which employers and professional people would have more votes than those lower down the social hierarchy.

The political philosopher D. D. Raphael (1916–) is startled to discover that John Stuart Mill felt it necessary to defend liberty *against* democracy, and Mill tells us in the *Autobiography* that, while he had become a socialist, he was less of a democrat than he had been. Macpherson concedes that, in arithmetical terms, Mill stepped back from the position of his father and Bentham. By this Macpherson means that Mill had reservations about one person, one vote, although he favoured a deeper involvement from those politically engaged. It has to be said that not only was John Stuart Mill worried that democracy would bring about what he called 'class legislation', he also argued (with India in mind) that despotism is 'a legitimate mode of governing barbarians'.

The new liberals and democracy

The problem with Macpherson's argument is that it underplays the real tensions between liberalism and democracy. This tension continues even when liberals are persuaded by the case for universal suffrage. Hobhouse, a pioneer of new liberalism, described democracy as 'the necessary basis of the liberal idea'. He warns of the dangers imperialism might pose for liberties at home — 'a democrat cannot be a democrat for his country alone' — but he could not make up his mind as to whether to support home rule for the Irish. He invokes an old liberal prejudice against dependents and servants by arguing that as far as the Crown colonies are concerned, it may be that a 'semi-despotic system' is the best that can be devised. He warns that the doctrine of popular sovereignty might lead to the 'expropriation of the rich', and he sees the suspensive veto of a second chamber and the use of referendums as valuable devices to check a 'large and headstrong majority'.

T. H. Green (1836–82), also a new liberal, saw in the 'true state' a community-based organ that would obliterate the interests of class, and he followed Rousseau in stressing the importance of religion to social order. Just as Hobhouse had considered independent peasants to be 'the backbone of the working population', so Green saw the mainstay of social contentment as residing with 'a class of small proprietors tilling their own land'. Although Green advocated universal suffrage, he was biased towards property.

Macpherson is surely right to argue that what reduced the extent of the franchise was imperial expansion, which had the effect of making ordinary voters in colony-owning countries feel that they indeed had a stake in the community. But this suggests that the easy equation of liberalism and democracy needs to be resisted, since the old concern that liberalism is about property rights, and not popular power, is never far below the surface. Guido di Ruggiero (1888–1949), an admirer of Hobhouse, argued that the term 'liberal' qualifies the term 'democratic'. He took the view that liberals must choose their recruits from among those who understand the value of freedom, human personality and autonomy; who are independent, respect the law and are self-critical; who can realise the dominion of thought over the inferior activities of the mind. These distinguished beings are naturally the middle classes.

Schumpeter's 'redefinition' of democracy

After the Second World War, a reaction set in against what were seen as the woolly and abstract ideals of the liberal tradition. An irreverence developed, which demanded that students of politics confront the world as it really is. Macpherson seems enthusiastic about this. He finds in the 'equilibrium model' (as he calls it) pioneered by Joseph Schumpeter (1883–1950) a substantially accurate description of how the Western liberal system actually works. This model is based upon the careful and extensive empirical investigation of a whole host of competent scholars.

In *Capitalism, Socialism and Democracy* (1943), Schumpeter argues that democracy has nothing to do with ideals. We should stop thinking in ethical terms, since there is nothing desirable as such about a democracy. Indeed, it may be that in some situations — Schumpeter instances the religious settlement under the military dictatorship of Napoleon I —the wishes of the people are more fully realised when there is no democracy.

In Schumpeter's view, democracy is simply a 'political method'. It is an arrangement for reaching political decisions, not an end in itself. Since all governments 'discriminate' against some section of the population (in no political system are children allowed to vote, for example), discrimination as such is not undemocratic. It all depends upon how you define the demos (i.e. the people). Schumpeter accepts that in contemporary liberal societies all adults should have the right to vote, but this does not mean that they will use this right or participate more directly in the political process. In fact, he argues that it is better if the mass of the population does not participate, since the masses are too irrational, emotional, parochial and 'primitive' to make good decisions.

The typical citizen, Schumpeter argues, yields to prejudice, impulse and what he calls 'dark urges'. It is the politicians who raise the issues that determine peoples' lives, and who decide these issues. Democracy is more realistically defined as a political method by which politicians are elected through a competitive vote. The people do not rule: their role is to elect those who do. Democracy is therefore a system of elected and competing elites.

The equilibrium model

The 1950s saw a number of studies which argued that politics is a remote, alien and unrewarding activity best left to a relatively small number of professional activists. Elected leadership should be given a free hand, since 'where the rational citizen seems to abdicate, nevertheless angels seem to tread'. The model of elitist democracy, as this idea has sometimes been called, presented the case for a democracy with low participation.

The realism espoused by political scientists in the 1950s and 1960s is highly problematic. How accurate was the model of liberal democracy that the realists developed? Macpherson's critique of the equilibrium model is of particular interest here.

Postwar liberals liked to present their redefined concept of democracy as an exchange process — a market model with voters as the consumers and politicians as the entrepreneurs. However, as Macpherson points out, this exercise in political realism assumes a state of perfect competition, an optimum distribution of political energies and goods. But reality is much more oligarchical than the realists assume. On the supply side, a small number of sellers (the competing party leaderships) can manipulate demand, while on the demand side, the more resources consumers have, the more vigorously they can express their preferences. The higher socioeconomic classes can participate much more cost-effectively than the lower classes.

The problem of apathy

Macpherson speaks of a 'class differential in apathy'. The liberal realists had argued that non-participation by the masses was good for democracy, but Macpherson argues that this apathy is not 'natural' and in fact the product of inequality. A more egalitarian distribution of wealth, the provision of better education, healthcare and welfare, and encouraging people to participate in the decision-making process would begin to dispel the 'dark urges' and irrational impulses that paralyse the political capacity of the mass of the population.

What the liberal realists are truly espousing is not greater realism but the cynicism of those who, having formulated ideals in a rather abstract way, now reject them with a world-wise weariness. The elitists, in the words of David Held (1951–), are 'liberals in despair'. A huge irony occurs. What were once liberal criticisms of democracy become the prerequisites of democracy itself. Schumpeter was to complain that the electorate was incapable of any action other than a stampede, and urged that a ban be placed on the practice of bombarding members of parliament with letters and telegrams.

Liberalism and realism

Robert Dahl (1915–), who had done much to develop a realist model, came to argue in his later work *Democracy and its Critics* (1989) that democracy should be seen as 'a daring vision' that forever invites us to look beyond and break through existing limits. But as far as the realists were concerned, democracy was the liberal status quo and anything that challenged this was a threat to democracy. Crick had argued that politics needed defending against democracy, since the trouble with communists, for example, was that they did not merely *pretend* to be democratic, they *were* democratic, and democracy could devour rather than enhance the freedom of the individual.

For the realists, on the other hand, there is a sharp antithesis between the democracy of the free world and the 'totalitarianism' of the communist one. Critics referred to this view as 'cold war liberalism', and in 1962 Giovanni Sartori (1924–), an Italian writer steeped in US political science, referred to the need for 'expert and accountable elites' to save democracy from 'the excesses of perfectionism, the vortex of demagogy'. The demagogy that had once characterised democracy (in the eyes of its traditional liberal critics) now negated it.

| Table 3.1 | The relationship between liberalism and democracy |

Classical liberals	Benthamite liberals	New liberals	Revisionist liberals
Natural rights	Utility	Development	Elitism
Democracy not an issue	Cautious support for democracy	More enthusiastic but still reservations	Rule by experts

Conclusion

Although liberals spoke of freedom and equality as basic to humans, it is wrong to assume that this automatically meant support for democracy. It was only in the twentieth century that liberals began to support democracy, and even then with considerable reservations. In the USA, which Tocqueville believed embodied democracy, the Founding Fathers were liberals rather than democrats, and popular rule there was premised upon an unusually wide spread of property rights. It is true that critics of liberalism based their arguments upon the assumptions of the liberal tradition, arguing that if all were free and equal, why did not this include women and workers etc.? But liberalism and democracy are different concepts, and the notion that the word 'liberal' can qualify the word democracy (i.e. 'liberal democracy') puts the matter well.

After the Second World War a number of theorists redefined democracy in ways that presented what they considered to be a more realistic view of the concept. Liberalism was deemed compatible with a form of elitism that left politicians, once they are elected by the masses, free to make decisions on their own.

Summary

- Liberalism and democracy should not be taken as synonyms. Historically, liberals were hostile to democracy even though their conservative critics accused them of being democratic.
- The founders of the US Constitution were liberal republicans rather than democrats, and even Jefferson, who is often regarded as a great democrat, was in fact a liberal who felt that only male property owners should have the vote.
- What created the tension between liberalism and democracy was the concern for property rights. The USA was unusual in that large sections of the people owned property, so it appeared to be a democratic society (unless you were a slave or a Native American).
- Tocqueville's analysis of US society in the 1830s confused democracy with liberalism. Although he was struck by the relatively high levels of equality, Tocqueville noted that

sections of business were becoming more and more concentrated, and class divisions were arising on US soil.

- With the rise of the robber barons after the civil war (1861–65), the US republic became sharply plutocratic (i.e. ruled by the rich). Ironically, democracy was declared to be a synonym for capitalism, and only occasionally did the old liberal suspicion of democracy surface.

- Macpherson notes the tension between liberalism and democracy, but his notion that Rousseau and Jefferson were 'one-class democrats' is superficial and inaccurate. With the rise of utilitarianism, class divisions were openly acknowledged. The concept of natural rights was dropped, but Bentham and James Mill took the view that universal male suffrage could be established and property rights still be protected.

- John Stuart Mill not only reacted against his father's version of utilitarianism, he felt that class divisions made representative government more problematic than Bentham and James Mill had assumed. He favoured giving people with property more votes, but even when liberals accepted 'one man, one vote' they still expressed reservations about popular majorities and sovereign legislatures.

- After the Second World War, Joseph Schumpeter developed a 'revisionist' view of democracy that saw decision making not as the responsibility of the people, but of an elected elite. Liberals, in the name of 'realism', constructed what Macpherson calls an equilibrium model of democracy. Democracy is based on a perfectly competitive market, with mass apathy and low rates of participation.

- What had been considered weaknesses of democracy — e.g. perfectionism, majoritarian tyranny — now become problems that a realistic model of democracy can avoid.

Task 3.1

Using this chapter and other resources available to you, answer the following questions:

1 Why are liberals often mistaken for democrats?

2 Why did Tocqueville call the USA a democratic society?

3 What accounts for the tension between liberalism and democracy?

4 Is it fair to characterise liberalism as an essentially middle-class philosophy?

5 Is 'democratic elitism' a rejection of liberal principles?

Guidance

Question1

Historically liberals were not democrats. They were concerned with the rights of property and those who owned property, and they feared that granting political rights to the mass of the population would undermine these rights and cause instability. Because they championed the free market, they took the view that those who were poor might use political power to increase taxes so that the state provided what

Task 3.1 (continued)

middle class individuals could provide for themselves. If healthcare and education, for example, were publicly funded, this would inevitably distort the free market, increase state intervention and undermine the kind of independence liberals felt was essential to human wellbeing.

Yet liberals were accused of being democrats by their conservative opponents. Why? The answer lies in the way liberals expressed their beliefs. They took the view that all men are free and equal, that they are rational and wish to govern their own lives, and conservative opponents interpreted this to mean that the mass of the population should enjoy democratic rights. Liberal abstractions were taken at face value and assumed to be concrete assertions. If liberals in the eighteenth century said that all men had natural rights, this must mean that everyone should be able to vote, stand for parliament and have the same resources.

A further conservative fear was that liberals were vulnerable to exploitation by what was later to be called the 'left'. Had not the English Civil War, the aftermath of the US War of Independence, and, above all, the Terror that followed the French Revolution demonstrated that liberal values could be used to extend power and resources to the detriment of 'civilisation' and 'order'? Liberals were not democrats until the twentieth century, but they expressed their values in universal and formally egalitarian terms, and this could lead to confusion and 'exploitation'.

Question 2

Tocqueville, a French aristocrat with liberal leanings, was fascinated by the USA in the late 1830s and early 1840s. His *Democracy in America* was a detailed account of its political, social and cultural institutions. Because of Tocqueville's conservatism, he tended to see democratic potential in liberal mores, and there is no doubt that the USA was the most liberal society of its time.

Because the country had not developed through a wholesale attack on a feudal order its liberalism was astonishingly 'pure'. Moreover, the wide distribution of property meant that the mass of the population took part in government, even though they were imbued with liberal republicanism rather than democratic ideology. Tocqueville assumed that because Americans believed passionately in freedom and equality they must be democrats, although he himself noted that women did not have the vote, black people were enslaved in the south and Native Americans had had their lands seized in a most shameful and violent manner.

As a liberal conservative Tocqueville equated the market with democracy, and although he noted the sharp differences between French radicals and US liberals it never occurred to him to see the USA as a relatively egalitarian liberal republic rather than as a liberal democracy.

Task 3.1 (continued)

Question 3

Liberals identified freedom and equality with the rights of property owners. They assumed that individuals were educated, affluent, independent, cultured, and (until the end of the nineteenth century) men rather than women. Liberals in the seventeenth and eighteenth centuries also took the view that individuals were not only Christians, but Protestants as well. Catholicism was seen as a medieval religion that was riddled with superstition, and Catholics had shown themselves to be unreliable supporters of independent nation states like Britain and Holland.

Democracy was seen as a dangerous and unworkable idea that encouraged people with no property to imagine that they were able to govern. Even in the USA, 'democracy' was seen as a problematic idea and was to constitute simply one branch within a balanced constitution. Even when liberals supported the extension of the franchise, they did so in the belief that ordinary people would follow middle-class leadership, so that those who were involved in government remained wealthy, educated and middle class. Although liberalism expressed itself in universal terms, the notion of the 'people' and the 'individual' referred to particular kinds of people, and was not intended to embrace the mass of the population.

Even today, neoliberals only support democracy provided it strengthens the market and capitalism. Where democratic rule undermines these institutions, neoliberals would prefer more autocratic forms of rule.

Question 4

Historically liberalism was the ideology of the middle classes. 'Middle class' means people opposed to the monopolies and privileges that characterised feudal and absolute monarchies — people whose lifestyle as lawyers, writers, financiers (later industrialists), craftsmen and farmers encouraged a sense of independence and a belief that success came from an ability to follow self-interest. Liberalism appealed to property owners who had acquired their wealth through hard work and a willingness to defer present gratification in order to obtain rewards in the future.

But to say liberalism is an essentially middle-class philosophy does not take sufficient account of the universal character of liberal values. It is true that natural rights theory and individualism were intended to apply to people of wealth and independence, but this did not prevent others from pushing liberal abstractions so that they became more concrete in character. If men were individuals, why not women too? If people with property could enjoy political rights, why couldn't workers? If liberals argued for toleration, why should this not extend to people who had other religions, or indeed none at all?

Task 3.1 (continued)

To say that liberalism is a middle-class philosophy is partly true, but it ignores the way liberalism raises questions and offers challenges that enable others to apply to society and make concrete relatively abstract propositions and values.

Question 5

'Democratic elitism' arose in the period immediately after the Second World War and presented its case in terms of realism. Liberal views of democracy had traditionally been woolly and idealistic, it was argued, and a much more hard-headed approach was required. Liberal realists believed it was not a question of what people ought to do, but what they actually did, and saw their new approach as scientific and empirical, not normative and evangelical.

The universal and abstract dimension of traditional liberalism was attacked, and the argument advanced that in democracies it was not the case that the people ruled, but rather that the people — or those who chose to exercise their political rights — elected politicians who took the decisions. The people who really counted were minorities. However, unlike the elitists proper, 'democratic elitists' insisted that people should have political rights and traditional liberal freedoms should be preserved. Nevertheless, communist and fascist rule had shown that majorities can act in ways that were seen as 'primitive' and authoritarian — perhaps ironically, democracies flourished where relatively few people participated and even fewer took decisions.

'Democratic elitism' involved a narrowing rather than a rejection of liberal principles. It was a relatively conservative interpretation of liberalism — a form of democracy that kept people at bay but did not deny them a role altogether.

Useful websites

- www.en.wikipedia.org/wiki/Liberalism
- www.liberalsindia.com/introduction/liberalpositionpapers/liberalpositionpapers3.php

Further reading

- Crick, B. (1982) *In Defence of Politics*, Penguin.
- Dahl, R. (1989) *Democracy and its Critics*, Yale University Press.
- Hoffman, J. (1988) *State, Power and Democracy*, Wheatsheaf.
- Macpherson, C. B. (1977) *The Life and Times of Liberal Democracy*, Oxford University Press.
- Tocqueville, A. de *Democracy in America*.

Chapter 4

Is the UK a liberal democracy?

The UK regards itself as a liberal democracy, but how liberal and how democratic is it? In answering this question, we will look at arguments that the capitalist nature of British society impairs its democratic character, as well as assessing the problem the state poses for democracy. Has the development of international terrorism and Britain's involvement in the conflict in Iraq impacted negatively on the liberal character of British political institutions?

Miliband and pluralism

Chapter 3 noted the development of a 'revised' notion of liberal democracy that reduced democracy to the election of decision-making elites. In the late 1960s the volume of criticism of liberal democracy escalated, much of it Marxist in inspiration. As early as 1964 Herbert Marcuse brought out his *One Dimensional Man*, which argued that capitalism and the socialism of Communist Party states had depoliticised the public so that its members became mere pawns in the grip of bureaucrats and manipulators. Even earlier (in 1956) C. Wright Mills contended in *The Power Elite* that liberal democracies were run by an unholy alliance of big business, bureaucrats and the military establishment.

But it was Ralph Miliband's *The State in Capitalist Society* (1969) that made a major impact. Dedicated to the memory of C. Wright Mills, this book argued that in liberal democracies an economically dominant class exercises decisive political power. A combination of state administrators sympathetic to capitalism from within and structural pressures from without neutralises any government mandated by its electors to introduce radical change. The pluralism of Western liberal democracies is much more limited than it appears. Civil servants, media tycoons, party leaders and the captains of industry enjoy a common social background, so, although there is competition, it takes place within the consensus that a capitalist society is natural and inevitable.

The problem of bourgeois democracy

Miliband accepts that societies such as that of the UK have liberal democratic political institutions and that they are characterised by political competition between parties, regular elections, representative assemblies, civil guarantees, a free press, and so on. Civil and political liberties are important. They affect materially the encounter between state and citizen, but they are 'bourgeois' freedoms within a 'bourgeois democracy', since the whip hand is exercised by business and financial elites who constitute a 'ruling class'.

His work is a detailed analysis of how dominant power is exercised through democratic institutions. The state elites — the civil service, judiciary, army and police — are (often unwittingly) sympathetic to capitalist interests, and the education sector and media serve to legitimise capitalist institutions, however much teachers and journalists may believe they are devoted to the pursuit of the truth. The Conservatives, Liberal Democrats and Labour reinforce this capitalist status quo (albeit in different ways), and radical ideas, even radical election manifestos, are neutralised by institutional pressures. The system may be democratic, but it operates in the interests of the bourgeoisie.

'Parliamentarism'

In *Capitalist Democracy in Britain* (1982) Miliband notes that universal suffrage was introduced into the UK in the nineteenth and twentieth centuries, with women obtaining the vote in 1918 and 1928 (see Box 4.1). In his view, the UK is outstanding for the way in which pressures and conflicts have been smoothly contained. Reforms have served to prevent social unrest. Miliband does not deny that members of the state elite differ in their functions and responsibilities from business and financial elites, but his point is that a common social and educational background binds them together. Differences in wealth, income, conditions of work, security, education, housing, health and 'life chances' in general are substantial between the classes, and the UK is not one nation, as ideologists contend. Elites therefore prevent potential class conflict.

The political climate is dominated by what Miliband calls 'parliamentarism' — the belief that all change must come through the Commons, whose rituals and milieu have tended to tame even the most radical of members. The prime minister exercises substantial powers of patronage, and rebels and critics are co-opted into higher posts. A belief in parliament runs through the political spectrum, with the exception of the extreme left and right.

> **Box 4.1**
> **The franchise in Britain**
>
> **1832** Reform Act gives middle-class males the vote.
> **1867** Second Reform Act extends the franchise to male town householders.
> **1884** Third Reform Act extends the vote to agricultural workers.
> **1918** Vote extends to women over 30 and all men over 21 (except lunatics, peers and prisoners).
> **1928** All women over 21 receive the vote.

The containment of pressure

In *Capitalist Democracy in Britain* Miliband also argues that trade unions play the role of 'routinising' conflict, and in this way act as valuable allies of the establishment. In the major political parties, but particularly Labour, political leaders seek to dampen the ardour and radicalism of 'activists'. Miliband concedes that the media does not explicitly propagate partisan views, but it plays a seminal role nevertheless in forging a capitalist 'hegemony' (i.e. a climate of opinion, a dominant set of values), while intellectuals are in general committed to 'moderation'. Governments, he argues, operate as the allies of capitalist enterprise, and the role of the public sector is to service the private one.

The state (as opposed to the elected government) functions to ensure a conservative continuity, and its passion for secrecy helps keep democratic pressures at bay. The police and the military contribute to this task, their role being much more restrained than it is in colonial situations or in relation to Ireland. The background of judges is not conducive to radicalism, and Miliband instances cases in which judges have ruled against militant trade unions and reformist local councils. The House of Lords is a highly conservative chamber, while the monarchy seeks to reduce working class alienation from the political and social system. In general, the political system has great capacity to absorb crisis, conflict and dislocation.

Macpherson's loopholes

In Macpherson's view, countries like the UK may be liberal democracies, but they are not very democratic. Macpherson is anxious to avoid the criticism that he is a mere utopian who hopes that, somehow or other, existing political systems can

become fairer (utopians hold fanciful and unrealistic views). He argues that there are three loopholes in the vicious circle of apathy and inequality.

The first loophole through which the system can become more democratic is the environment. Macpherson takes people to be self-interested consumers. To be a consumer, you must be able to undertake leisure activities safely, and if rivers and seas are polluted, for example, then this is not possible. In order to remain a self-interested consumer, involvement in an ecological movement becomes crucial.

Macpherson moves from the physical environment to problems with the social environment (the second loophole): inner-city decay, the ravages of property developers, ill-planned housing estates etc. People need to participate in dealing with these in order to continue their chosen life-style.

The third loophole relates to conditions at work. Growing insecurity, pension worries and lack of involvement in decision-making necessitate greater interest in the political process. This is not because there has been a miraculous conversion to politics, but because people cannot remain consumers unless they show an interest in a deteriorating world. Macpherson's argument is that the movement beyond the 'equilibrium' market-based model does not depend upon a sudden change in human nature.

Democratic political control

What adds to the realism of Macpherson's argument for a more participatory system is his view that a revolution, as conventionally defined, is not necessary to achieve it. Indeed, he argues that a revolution would actually work against the establishment of democratic political control, on the grounds that a revolutionary upheaval creates a sharp cleavage between revolutionaries and counter-revolutionaries, inevitably leading not to the spread of power, but to its centralisation. Such is the lesson of the 1917 October Revolution in Russia.

Macpherson formulated democratic models that overcome these problems. His Model A is the most realistic of these, since it argues for a pyramid of councils, in which people elect representatives at neighbourhood level, who would then send delegates to a local level, which in turn would have representatives at a regional and national level. The party system would remain as a way of ensuring debate and argument, whereas in his Model 4B, parties would no longer exist.

There is also, in my view, a strong case for compulsory voting on the grounds that participation is a duty as well as a right. It is true that people can and do participate in single-issue organisations like Amnesty International, but voting in elections in important. It should not only be encouraged but become mandatory. Ballot papers could easily include a box for 'none of the above' so that dissidents could be comfortably accommodated.

The problem of inequality

The postwar UK is an unequal society. The wealthiest quarter of the population owns about three quarters of the wealth, with about one fifth of the population living in poverty. Does this matter? Robert Dahl argued in *Who Governs?* (1961) that inequalities were 'dispersed', so a person without economic resources might still be influential politically, provided parties were competitive, there were regular elections, a free press and so on. This view has been severely criticised in a substantial body of literature, of which Steven Lukes's *Power: A Radical View* (1974) is the best example.

Not only can it be argued that the notion of 'dispersed inequalities' is superficial, but there is evidence to suggest that people are much more likely to join a political party, vote and participate generally, if they are educated, and have the resources, self confidence and verbal skills that go with this. In other words, inequalities in wealth translate broadly into inequalities in political power. An unequal society is less democratic than a more equal one.

It is difficult to avoid the startling fact that fewer and fewer people vote in elections. Turnout in 1997 in the UK was 59.4%, and this only increased to 61.3% in 2001. This means that some 40% of the population is governed by laws that it has played no part in shaping. The UK's major political institutions — the civil service, army, judiciary, police, executive and legislature — are still led by people educated at public schools. Although MPs have been paid since 1911, their links with financial institutions in the City continue, and account for the considerable influence financial interests have on British policy making.

Peculiar British problems: the electoral system

In the UK there is the particular problem of the first-past-the-post (FPTP) system. In 1983, for example, the Liberal Democrats won 25.4% of the vote but only received 3.5% of the seats. In 1951 and 1974, the party that won the most seats won fewer votes than its rival. In FPTP a candidate only needs more votes than his or her rivals, and this might mean that in a four-way contest the winner receives little more than a quarter of the votes cast. It is calculated that, because

of the way constituency boundaries are drawn, had the Conservatives won 43.2% of the vote in the 1997 election (instead of Labour) and Labour won 30.7% (instead of the Conservatives), the Conservative majority would have been 45, whereas in fact Labour's majority was 172.

The use of a type of proportional representation (PR) in the 1999 Scottish Parliament elections meant Labour had to form a coalition with the Liberal Democrats, and Labour formed a minority administration in Wales in the same year. Under PR, voters can vote for the party they genuinely prefer without worrying about a wasted vote. It could certainly be argued that British political institutions would be more democratic with a fairer electoral system, though of course champions of the present system stress that stability and decisiveness are more likely to prevail where candidates in single-member constituencies simply need more votes than their rivals to win.

The 'elective dictatorship'

In 1978 the late Lord Hailsham used the term 'elective dictatorship' to describe the power that a government has in parliament. The leader of a majority party can do more or less what he or she wants, using the whips in the House of Commons to ensure that MPs vote according to the leader's demands.

This is a peculiarly British situation. The separation of powers between the legislature and the executive does not really operate in the UK: the prime minister is an MP, and the members of the cabinet are also members of parliament, usually of the Commons. Since there is no written constitution, the argument is that a prime minister can carry through policies that bear little relationship to the 'promises' made in the manifesto on which the party was elected. Legislation from the EU, court powers of intervention and the probing of investigative journalism constitute relatively weak constraints on the executive. It could be said that the parliamentary, cabinet and prime ministerial system is a limitation on the democratic process.

The House of Lords

The UK is the only country in the world to have an unelected second chamber in its parliament. It is true that in 1911 and 1949 parliament passed acts to restrict the Lords' power of delay over bills from the Commons, and by convention it does not oppose measures that have been in the election manifesto of the government.

But the Lords remains an anomaly, and it is clear that the planned reforms of the present Labour government do not redress this. Under the reforms, the Lords will become a chamber of 600 and the hereditary element will be abolished. But the number of members actually elected will be restricted to 120, with a further 120 nominated by a statutory commission and the rest allocated to political parties in proportion to the vote they achieve in the general election. The seats occupied by bishops would be reduced from 25 to 16.

While these reforms make the Lords more democratic, they fall short of extending the elective principle to the whole of the second chamber. The House of Lords remains a body that is inconsistent with democratic principles.

The conflict in Iraq

In 2003 the British government joined the government in the USA in going to war in Iraq. This has been extremely controversial, with opponents arguing that the action was illegal because it obtained no endorsement from the United Nations, and the government in the UK conceding that the weapons of mass destruction supposedly possessed by Iraq do not in fact exist. Not only has the UK's involvement in the war weakened substantially the prime minister's stature and authority, but it has been bad for the development of democracy in the UK.

A mass demonstration in London against the government's stance on Iraq, February 2003

The Iraq conflict has generated cynicism among the general public towards formal politics, since the enormous demonstration against the war in February 2003 appeared to have no effect on the government. Second, it has exacerbated the sense of vulnerability that arose after the atrocities in the USA in 2001, and this has led to large numbers of arrests and detentions. There is evidence that the UK's liberal institutions have been eroded as a result of the fear of terrorism, and it is argued by critics of the Iraq conflict that the bombings in London in July 2005 would not have taken place had the UK not been involved in the US action.

Security and secrecy

All liberal democratic states operate with a degree of secrecy in combating their enemies, yet the British state seems to be unusually secretive. MI5, the domestic intelligence service, is not accountable to parliament but under the control of the home secretary. The Official Secrets Act (1989) has a controversial Section 2 that makes it a crime for state employees to pass on information to those not authorised to have it. This is one of a number of laws and institutions — including the power to tap the phones of supposed subversives, preventing the release of information for 30 years, and the existence of a General Communications Headquarters for coding and decoding — that makes the UK one of the more secretive states in the Western world.

It is noteworthy that the New Labour government has not significantly liberalised access of information, as was hoped: the Freedom of Information Act (2000) makes a number of welcome changes, but arguably none of these are substantial.

The Troubles in Northern Ireland

Until the late 1960s mainland Britain tolerated a situation in Northern Ireland in which the Catholic minority was subject to systematic discrimination in the allocation of housing, the provision of jobs, and the boundaries for local elections. In 1969 British troops were sent to the province because of the eruption of violence; in 1972 direct rule from Westminster was imposed, and the regional parliament at Stormont, just outside Belfast, was suspended.

It could be argued that Ulster has compromised the liberal democratic credentials of British governments since 1922, when Lloyd George negotiated a Treaty of Partition that established a six-county Northern Ireland, excluding three counties of the historic Ulster. In 1971 the Stormont government imposed an internment in which substantial numbers of relatively non-political Catholics were subject to human rights abuses, and 2 years after direct rule was introduced the British parliament passed a Prevention of Terrorism Act (1974) in response to the Irish Republican Army's (IRA) bombing campaign in mainland Britain.

The Troubles have not been good for liberal democracy in Britain. Thirteen people were shot dead in the Bloody Sunday demonstration in 1972, and 9 years later ten Republican prisoners died in a hunger strike. It was only in 1997 that the British government sought to negotiate directly with representatives from the violent wing of the republican movement, recognising that it was futile and counterproductive to try to secure a military victory over the IRA. The situation in Northern Ireland has aggravated the tendency to secrecy and corruption in the state machine so that the UK's standing as a liberal democracy has suffered as a consequence.

Joining the European Union

In 1972 the UK joined what was then the European Common Market. Opponents and critics of the European Union (EU) argue that the UK's membership has led to a surrender of national sovereignty, radically under-mining the democratic status of the British polity. The European Court of Justice has established the superiority of European law over British law; qualified majority voting in the Council of Ministers has eroded the British veto; and the Maastricht Treaty (which John Major signed in 1992) has extended the powers of the EU. With New Labour accepting the Social Chapter of this treaty, EU powers over British labour regulations have been further extended.

But it could be argued that the EU does not erode British democracy, since the UK has its share of European commissioners and British voters elect members to the European Parliament. Moreover, in my view state sovereignty is an incoherent concept, and it might well be that the UK has in fact become more influential and prosperous as a result of EU membership. Supporters of the EU speak of 'shared sovereignty' and thus contest vigorously the suggestion that the EU has weakened British democracy. Indeed, a case could be made arguing that the EU's powers are too limited.

At the moment European citizens must be citizens of member states, and there is a 'democratic deficit' with regard to the secrecy and privacy of the Council of Ministers that acts on behalf of member states. Relatively few people vote in European elections, and giving the European Parliament more powers might increase the sense of popular involvement in European institutions.

The 'tyranny thesis'

There is a wider problem with liberal democracy that does not only affect the UK. It has been argued that elections cause a tyranny of the majority to arise that can act in an illiberal way and persecute minorities. Certainly this is a danger, and it has already become apparent that a climate of opinion can easily be created and laws passed that arguably exacerbate rather than reduce problems, for example the danger of terrorism.

But this is not a problem, as is sometimes suggested, with democracy itself, but with an approach that looks at people as isolated individuals. These individuals, it is argued, can be free and act democratically, even if they act in a way that harms other individuals. In my view, this is the wrong way to assess the question of democracy. People are related to one another whether they are aware of this or not, so the lack of democracy for some affects democracy for all.

The Troubles in Northern Ireland are a case in point. The 'tyranny' that prevailed before 1972 affected democracy for everyone, since the ascendant Protestants had their freedom undermined by the fear and insecurity that the 'Protestant state for the Protestant people' generated. All British people suffer from the intolerance and prejudice that the conflict in Iraq is generating. The problem lies not with too much democracy, but too little.

The problem of the state

The UK, like most other countries, has a state. Peoples who do not have a state, like the Kurds, tend to aspire to them. States are so common in the world we forget it could be argued that there is considerable tension between the idea of a liberal democracy and the concept of the state. According to the definition of the German sociologist Max Weber (1864–1920), the state is an institution that claims a monopoly of legitimate force for a particular territory. But why is this definition in tension with the idea of liberal democracy?

A liberal democracy is a society in which people govern their own lives. States are institutions that use force to settle conflicts of interest, and the use of force prevents people from governing their own lives. In 2003 there were 73,000 prisoners in England and Wales, but force affects far more than simply those who are put in prison. The use of force to settle conflicts of interest generates what I would call a 'statist' mentality, so that moral and social pressures (which can be effective in settling conflicts) are pushed to one side, and coercion is regarded as the way of handling disputes.

The UK is a relatively tolerant society, but the existence of the state can exacerbate the problems of secrecy and elitism that bedevil a liberal democracy. It is true that when conflicts of interest cannot be resolved by social and moral sanctions the use of force is inevitable, but we should be aware of how force affects quality of life in society as a whole. The use of force can often be counter-productive, encouraging short-term solutions to long-term problems and creating resentment and injustice. The more the UK relies on force to tackle conflicts of interest, the less democratic it becomes.

Conclusion

Liberal democracy in general has been criticised for failing to practise what it preaches. Instead of representing the interests of the people as a whole, it serves the interests of a capitalist class, and in the UK an ideology of parliamentarism, the media and the education system further serve to present capitalist values as a 'common sense'. The system can only become more democratic if it becomes more egalitarian and participatory. This can be achieved without a revolution and through concern for the environment, both natural as well as social, and conditions of work.

A number of features make liberal democracy in the UK particularly problematic: the electoral system (it could be argued), the parliamentary system and an unelected House of Lords. The British state is unusually secretive, and this feature has not been helped by its conduct in Northern Ireland and involvement in the Iraq conflict. Critics of the European Union argue it has further threatened liberal democracy in the UK (though its supporters vigorously dispute this). However, those who contend that democracy itself is liable to become a 'tyranny of the majority' blame democracy for what is in fact a problem of the state — an elitist institution that tackles conflicts of interest through the use of force.

Summary

- The democratic character of liberal political systems in Western countries has been challenged by Marxists like Miliband, who argue that the pluralism of these systems is compromised by the existence of a ruling capitalist class. The state, whatever its claims to impartiality, and the government, despite its electoral mandate, pursue the interests of this class because of a common social background and the structural constraints imposed by business and financial institutions.
- In *Capitalist Democracy in Britain* Miliband undertakes a similar analysis of British political institutions, arguing that Labour governments in particular, whatever the character of their

election manifestos, enact policies that are necessarily and invariably pro-capitalist in character. An ideology of parliamentarism undermines any notion of systemic change, while the media and the education sector create a belief system that takes free enterprise for granted.

- Macpherson argues that apathy and inequality reinforce each other, but this vicious circle can be broken by a number of loopholes. A deteriorating natural and social environment, along with increasing insecurity at work, act to compel people to get involved in political processes.

- A more democratic system can be obtained without a revolution, and in a way that preserves the party system. Although people participate in single-issue pressure groups, there is also a case for not merely encouraging them to vote, but making it mandatory for parliamentary and local elections.

- The argument that inequalities can be 'dispersed' is not plausible. Inequality weakens the democratic character of political institutions, and the first-past-the-post system in the UK is, in the eyes of many, unfair. If proportionality is good enough for Scotland, Wales and Northern Ireland, then (it is argued) it is good enough for UK national elections.

- The particular parliamentary system in the UK operates to frustrate a healthy division between the executive and legislature, and the existence of a second chamber that is (despite recent reforms) still largely unelected is anomalous.

- The UK's involvement in the Iraq conflict has, its critics argue, worked against the development of liberal democracy, and the state in the UK is unnecessarily secretive. Its record in Northern Ireland has not, it is contended, shown British democracy in a particularly positive light. On the other hand, joining the European Union has, in the view of Europhiles, developed a more mature view of the UK's role in the world.

- Those who argue that democracy itself leads to a 'tyranny of the majority' have an outmoded view of individuals and fail to see that 'an injury to one is an injury to all'. The problem with liberal democracy in the UK, as elsewhere, is that the state itself weakens liberal and democratic norms with its divisive method for tackling conflicts of interest.

Task 4.1

Read the passage below and answer the questions that follow.

The monarchy

The UK has a hereditary monarchy, but it is argued that this is compatible with liberal democracy because the monarchy is 'constitutional'. Although the monarch is still called the sovereign, in fact this role is largely ceremonial and symbolic. The assent of the Crown is required to pass laws, and the monarch has the power to dissolve parliament and choose the prime minister.

These powers are largely formal. The monarch dissolves parliament on the instructions of the prime minister, and the leader of the party winning an election becomes

Task 4.1 (continued)

prime minister. Nevertheless, the formality of these powers should not be overstated. For example, in 1931 the Labour prime minister Ramsey MacDonald was unable to persuade many of his colleagues to introduce 'economy' measures; King George V played a key role in persuading MacDonald to form a national government, a move that left the Labour Party in the wilderness until after the Second World War.

It should be remembered that the monarch may acquire formidable political expertise and experience. In a crisis situation he or she can play a critical role, and given his/her wealth and position it is not difficult to guess which section of the political spectrum he/she inhabits. Critics argue that the monarch has become increasingly anomalous in a democratic, multicultural society, and the death of Princess Diana in 1997 revealed considerable popular disquiet about its existence. On the other hand, the monarch is seen as a central part of British pageantry and tradition, and far more satisfactory (and cost-effective) than a presidential head of state in a republic.

Discussion

Consider the arguments for and against the monarchy in the UK. Which of the three options below would you support and why?

1 The retention of the monarchy as it stands.

2 The reform and modernisation of the monarchy.

3 The abolition of the monarchy so that the UK becomes a republic.

Arguments in favour of the monarchy

- The monarchy has no real constitutional power. It can therefore concentrate on its symbolic role as head of state, acting as an important ambassador abroad and winning the admiration and affection of peoples throughout the world, and, in particular, the Commonwealth, where people formerly under colonial rule see the monarch as a source of inspiration and international affiliation.
- The monarchy is a symbol of national unity. It is an institution that generates national pride and goodwill, making people feel proud to be British. The monarchy does not merely represent the English; it embodies the aspirations of the people of Wales, Scotland and Northern Ireland as well. People feel that they belong to a 'united' kingdom. The system of honours involves recognition from the monarch and is an important incentive to ordinary people to work for the community.
- Because the monarch it not elected, it is independent of the pressures of party politics and can speak its mind fearlessly and directly. Through weekly meetings with the prime minister the monarch offers advice useful even to an experienced politician. It is possible for democracies to undertake foolish actions and pass ill-considered laws, and the monarchy can act as a healthy corrective to these excesses.
- The monarch acts as a magnet for overseas visitors, who pay substantial sums of money to see pageantry and tradition that they may not have in their native countries. A republican head of state would be expensive and much more controversial.

Task 4.1 (continued)

Arguments against the monarchy

- The notion that the monarchy has no political power is a myth. Where there is a political crisis, in which a cabinet is paralysed by dissent (as in 1931), an election is inconclusive or a ruling party loses its majority in parliament, the intervention by the monarch may be decisive.
- The fact the monarch does not belong to any particular political party does not mean that the king or queen is above politics. Monarchs are hugely wealthy and they are generally of the right rather than the left. They encourage caution and conservatism, so the monarchy acts as a brake upon the democratic process. From time to time members of the royal family express views that reveal the conservative nature of the institution.
- The monarchy is an archaic institution and woefully unrepresentative of British society. Most people are not wealthy, so from a class standpoint the monarchy is removed from the mass of the people. The monarch must be Anglican, even though he or she is to represent Nonconformists, Catholics, Jews, Muslims, Sikhs, atheists etc.
- The monarchy operates on a hereditary principle in an age where legitimacy should derive from election and accountability. It is wrong that a democratic country should have a head of state who is unelected, privileged, wealthy and unrepresentative.

Task 4.2

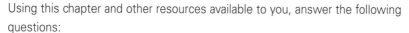

Using this chapter and other resources available to you, answer the following questions:

1 Does the existence of class divisions impair the democratic character of British political life?

2 Is the UK's electoral and parliamentary system in need of reform?

3 Why do significant numbers of people fail to vote, and is this a matter we should seek to rectify?

4 Is the UK's membership of the European Union a good thing for its status as a liberal democracy?

5 Consider the argument that the UK is as liberal and democratic as it is reasonable to expect it to be.

Guidance

Question 1

Democracy is a system of rule in which people govern their own lives. For this to be possible, people must feel confident and respected, articulate and critical-minded.

Task 4.2 (continued)

They must have the resources that enable a person to go to meetings and spend time campaigning and organising.

Class divisions work against this. Large numbers of people may be poorly educated, and class divisions allow some people to pay for their education, which is often (though not necessarily) superior to that provided by state schools. A class-divided society means that many people come from impoverished backgrounds and do not have the leisure time that political participation requires. They work in factories and offices where they are told what to do by others, so their self-esteem and confidence is continuously undermined. The division of society into rich and poor is bad for democracy, as it encourages arrogance and insensitivity from the 'haves' and indifference and ignorance from the 'have-nots'.

The argument that the concentration of wealth in relatively few hands is an economic rather than a political matter is not persuasive. Poverty is bad for a person's political as well as physical health, and inequality leads to cynicism, corruption and extremism. Class divisions create the kind of tensions that generate a 'statist' mentality — a belief that problems need to be suppressed through violence rather than addressed in a manner that seeks to understand and find solutions that will really help.

Democracy requires people to feel that they rely upon and serve the needs of others. Class divisions encourage selfishness and a short-term approach that creates problems for future generations.

Question 2

It is argued that the current electoral system provides stable government and a decisive result. The parliamentary system enables a party leader to be part of the legislative process, and cabinet government brings the executive under the control of members of parliament.

This system seems increasingly out of touch with contemporary social and political realities. People see themselves as individuals with a wide range of tastes and opinions: they want an electoral system that can register their desires, and although the proportional system has its difficulties it is hard to see how the current first-past-the-post system can continue in its present form. The adoption of PR for elections to the Welsh Assembly, the Scottish Parliament and the assembly in Northern Ireland indicates that it is not alien to British traditions.

As for the parliamentary system: not only does it seem to encourage polarised and adversarial politics, but pressures on parliamentarians and particularly on members of the cabinet make it much more difficult for people to speak their minds. Power is concentrated in the hands of the prime minister, who seems able to pursue policies

Task 4.2 (continued)

that are not favoured by members of his/her cabinet or MPs. A large majority makes a prime minister particularly powerful. Reforms that divide and disperse power are surely timely.

Question 3

The percentage of people voting is going down; in the USA, the proportion of the population voting in presidential elections is sometimes as low as 50%. This is clearly a problem, since laws apply to all and yet a substantial number of people play no part in electing the representatives who make these laws.

It was argued in the 1950s that non-participation was a good thing, since it left law making to the experts and high levels of voting could have authoritarian consequences. Besides, apathy denoted satisfaction, and was necessary for democracy to function. These arguments have rightly been contested. Apathy is not a good thing; although perhaps a tiny number of people do not vote because they are content with the laws made in their name, most people who do not vote lack confidence, resources and commitment. They are cynical about politicians, and a failure to vote may be followed by allegiance to extremist organisations. People who are prosecuted under the law are unlikely to have played any part in bringing the law about.

A number of policies can be pursued to reduce apathy. The first is for governments to concern themselves with the question of inequality, implementing measures that restrict the gap between rich and poor, and ensuring that resources are placed in the hands of those who most need them. John Stuart Mill's comment that government cannot do too much to help people help themselves is apposite here. Second, we need an electoral and representative system that encourages participation, so people feel that their wishes are meaningfully represented and that government is efficient and transparent.

Third, and perhaps most controversially, we need to redefine the meaning of citizenship, so that people not only have political rights, but an obligation to use them. There is much evidence that where voting is a legal requirement, far more people take part. Compulsory voting helps people to take citizenship seriously, and a ballot paper could easily be devised that allows people to vote for 'none of the above', should they feel that they do not like any of the candidates. Although this is a punitive policy, it should be linked to measures that both encourage and facilitate voting, with penalties as much moral as 'statist'.

Question 4

It is argued that the EU is progressing in a federalist direction, thus undermining the UK's position as an independent nation state and liberal democracy. Sovereignty is

Task 4.2 (continued)

being taken from the British parliament as more EU directives become law in the UK, and should these directives clash with British law it is European law that has supremacy. Conservatives who favoured an economic union fear that the EU's progression in a social and political direction is harmful for the UK's independence. Some members of the Labour Party still take the view that the EU blocks the kind of radical socialist change that the country requires.

This argument, however, assumes that the nation state is an eternal receptacle for liberal democracy. Why shouldn't democracy exist in regional and cosmopolitan forms? The EU is helping to modernise the UK and it can be argued that the EU contributes positively to the country's prosperity and influence in the world. Why not see sovereignty as linked to bodies much wider than the nation state, so that state sovereignty is 'pooled' in the EU, and the UK is more sovereign than it was before?

The European Parliament is not as influential as it could be and the EU should resist the temptation to present itself as a 'super state'. It is a new political arrange- ment — not an institution claiming a monopoly of legitimate force on a European scale. Of course, widening political horizons is a gradual process, and if Europhiles move too quickly this could strengthen nationalist reactions. But on balance, the UK's membership of the EU has been good for its status as a liberal democracy.

Question 5

The UK has many positive features. It is relatively stable, handles racial and ethnic questions in a reasonably enlightened fashion and has a parliamentary system that is still the envy of the world. It has undergone significant constitutional changes since the Labour Party came to office in 1997, so it could be argued that it is as liberal and democratic as it could be.

But this argument is rather complacent. It is true that the government and the media behaved well in response to the recent crisis over the publication of cartoons in Denmark that are offensive to Muslims, but the UK's participation in the Iraq conflict has angered Muslims (and many others), so relations with the Muslim minority are not good. There are disturbing signs that the government's reaction to the atrocities of 9/11 and the London bombings in July 2005 have weakened the UK's liberal traditions, and the response to the threat of terror has generally set back rather than advanced civil rights.

Electoral and political reforms have become more urgent, as the New Labour government is seen by many as increasingly autocratic in character, and the gap between rich and poor continues to grow. Measures to tackle environmental and transport problems are half-hearted, and the public services seem inadequate for the

Task 4.2 (continued)

twenty-first century. Among young people, there is considerable cynicism and escapism. British institutions have not been fully modernised: reform of the House of Lords has stalled and commitment to elections is declining.

While we should recognise the positive features of contemporary British politics, there is still much to be done to make the UK more liberal and democratic than it is at present.

Useful websites

- www.liberty-human-rights.org.uk

Further reading

- Budge, I. (et al.) (2001) *The New British Politics*, Longman.
- Lukes, S. (2005) *Power: a Radical View*, Palgrave.
- Miliband, R. (1969) *The State in Capitalist Society*, Weidenfeld and Nicolson.

Chapter 5

How liberal are the post-1997 constitutional reforms?

This chapter examines the liberal argument for devolution as part of the general liberal recognition of diversity. Can the liberal approach tackle successfully the issue of difference? Inevitably this raises further questions about democracy and the state.

The problem of sovereignty

Although Hobbes's *Leviathan* makes the case for state sovereignty, liberals are uneasy about the concept because it has monopolistic overtones and points to a concentration of power. Hobbes used the notion of the individual to suggest that the individual is sovereign over his (and it was 'his') life — in other words, all men have a natural right to self-preservation that nothing can take away. In the same way, the state is sovereign in that it represents all wills as one. But liberals have generally preferred to avoid concepts like sovereignty, sidelining them as necessary in an emergency, but unpalatable in terms of the give and take of everyday political life.

Locke tends to avoid the issue by implying that sovereignty might be 'shared' between the government and the people (i.e. male property owners), so that a state which transgresses the property rights of the people can be overthrown as a consequence. Liberals are not anarchists (although their conservative critics identify a strain of anarchism in the classical liberal view of the state). It is true that the state in classical liberalism is artificial, the product of contract, and viewed as a necessary evil, but it is a state nevertheless. In my view, liberals have

never been able to justify the notion of the state as embodying legitimate force, while at the same time arguing that force undermines, and is incompatible with, freedom.

Federalism and the state

Liberals have generally favoured a federalist over a unitary state. Federalism suggests dispersing power so that different sections of the polity all have some of it. The USA is the classic home of federalism, and it is greatly reluctant to describe any section of its society as 'sovereign'. The federal government has some power, but so do the states. The executive has power, but so do the legislature and the judiciary; the government has power, but so do the people. It is significant that, in general, the USA has been unwilling to subscribe to state-centric political theory, and some writers even (although in my view erroneously) refer to the USA as a stateless society.

The problem arises from the nature of force. Force implies concentration and monopoly: when force is used, one person or party succeeds only when the other is vanquished. Since federalist states use force to tackle conflicts of interest, they can be described as sovereign. When sovereignty was disputed during the US civil war, force was used on a terrifying scale to resolve the 'dispute'. Nevertheless, it remains the case that the more liberal the state, the less obvious the concentration of power, the greater the reluctance to use force, and the more vigorous the attempt to disperse sovereignty.

Nationalism and the UK

The UK has an ambivalent attitude towards nationalism. England, the dominant nation within the kingdom, conquered Wales in the sixteenth century and by 1707 had incorporated Scotland. Ireland was included in 1801. The practical strength of the Union has led to a historic indifference to the kind of nationalist symbolism powerful in the USA. It is revealing that only when the Union is deemed threatened — by joining the EU, for example, in the view of some — is it argued that the UK is a nation-state that Brussels weakens.

But a moment's reflection indicates how problematic the concept of the UK as a nation-state is. Are the British a nation, or are the English, Welsh and Scottish separate nations? Only on the far right or in Northern Ireland has the Union Jack been seen as an important emblem of unity, and that is because where unity is threatened it has to express itself symbolically. Historically, the

UK has been a unitary state — secure, self-confident and expansionist — with a liberalism that is closer to the centralism of Hobbes than the federalist orientation of Locke. 'Westminster' has been the unchallenged centre of the UK's political universe, with the people of the peripheries judging their success in terms of their ability to reproduce the values and lifestyle of the hegemonic southeast.

Liberalism and devolution

As an ideology of diversity and decentralisation, liberalism has taken root in 'peripheral' regions. It is revealing that the Liberal Party, now the Liberal Democrats, has traditionally drawn its electoral support from regions like Devon and Cornwall in the south and Scotland and Wales in the north and west — in other words, from areas where regionalism and minority nationalisms have been strongest. The regions have felt deprived of jobs and prosperity. During the 1950s, for example, a third of a million of Scots (out of a population of 5.5 million) left Scotland, half moving to the southeast and half going abroad.

New Labour came to power in 1997 with a reform programme that stressed the merits of greater devolution. It was clear to Labour that the centralisation which took place under Thatcherite conservatism (had not Thatcher said her favourite philosopher was Hobbes?) necessitated a break with the old Westminster-dominated model and significant constitutional reform. New Labour feared that, without such reform, nationalism in Scotland and Wales would grow and the demand for secession from the United Kingdom would increase. Northern Ireland had demonstrated that alienated minorities can turn to violent organisations if their aspirations are frustrated. Socialists therefore found a new inspiration and sympathy for liberal ideas of dispersal and diversity

The devolution agenda

The post of Welsh minister of state was created in 1957 and the minister received a position in the cabinet in 1964. In 1965 a Welsh office was established as a regional ministry handling questions of culture, the environment, local government, economic development and the like. In September 1997 a referendum on creating a Welsh Assembly was held in Wales that succeeded, although many Labour MPs in south Wales opposed the idea and only about a quarter of Welsh voters consider themselves more Welsh than British. The Welsh Assembly lacks the legislative powers of its Scottish counterpart, but it

was welcomed by Plaid Cymru, the Welsh nationalist party, which has pledged to fight for an increase in the assembly's powers.

Scotland is seen as far more distinctive than Wales. It has its own legal and education systems and its own media. As far back as 1882 a secretary of state for Scotland was created, and in 1895 this secretary had a seat in the cabinet. In 1928 a Scottish office was established. Around a third of voters support total independence and about the same proportion consider themselves more Scottish than British. There was more enthusiasm for a Scottish Parliament at the 1997 referendum than there had been for a Welsh Assembly. The Scottish Nationalist Party has welcomed the new parliament, which (unlike its Welsh counterpart) has minor tax-raising powers, and has continued to commit itself to Scottish independence.

In Northern Ireland things have been more difficult. A referendum in May 1998 established a power-sharing assembly with representatives from Sinn Fein (linked to the Irish Republican Army) and the Unionists. However, the Unionists have refused to share power with Sinn Fein.

Devolution has not only involved the Welsh, Scots and Northern Irish. In May 2000, presidential-style elections took place in Greater London to elect a mayor who, like the Scottish Parliament and Welsh Assembly, is willing to challenge the policies of the British government itself. Regional development agencies have been set up, but these consist of officials appointed by the government and are not representative. The defeat of a referendum in northeast England for a regional assembly suggests that there is no real appetite for regional government within England itself.

The Human Rights Act

In 1988 the UK Parliament passed the Human Rights Act (HRA), which brought the European Convention on Human Rights into UK domestic law. The convention was a treaty agreed to in 1950 but not made part of UK law.

The HRA changes the way we see ourselves as citizens and can be described as a piece of constitutional legislation in the tradition of Magna Carta (1215), the Bill of Rights (1688) that set up the constitutional monarchy, the Acts of Union with Scotland (1707) and Ireland (1800), the European Communities Act (1972), and the measures granting devolution detailed above.

The HRA applies to law in the past and laws that might be passed in the future. Unlike the common law, which allows a person to do anything that is not specifically banned, the HRA seeks to set out comprehensively what rights a person possesses. It is true that the courts cannot (as they can in the USA) strike down offending acts (i.e. acts that contravene the HRA) and deem them unconstitutional, but they can declare such acts 'incompatible' with the HRA. When new laws are made by the Commons, the relevant minister must present a statement of compatibility. The Anti-Terrorism, Crime and Security Act (2001) contravened the HRA in one of its clauses, and a 'derogation' (departure) had to be entered as a result. However, this derogation cannot be incompatible with international law.

It is unlawful for public authorities to contravene the HRA. Privacy is better protected than it was and damages or an injunction may result where such contravention has occurred. The right to be protected against pollution has been extended as a result of the HRA. The rights that the HRA entrenches are rights to life, personal security and liberty. Should there also be a right to work, social security and a good education?

The House of Lords

In July 2002 a committee was appointed to look into reform of the Lords. In 1999 the government decided to eliminate the hereditary principle, and all but 92 of the 750 hereditary peers were removed. Hereditary titles will continue to exist, but their holders will not in most cases be entitled to sit in the Lords. Lord Wakeham, who was asked by the government to examine the question of reform, argued for an appointments commission that would decide on the members of the Lords, thus taking away the power of the prime minister to appoint in this area.

Lord Wakeham discusses his proposals for reform of the House of Lords

The appointments commission is to have a statutory basis. It will choose members of the Lords in a way that emphasises the need to make the chamber representative of the UK in the twenty-first century. Law lords would no longer be members as a new Supreme Court is to be established. The Lords will become a chamber of 600, with the hereditary element abolished. But the numbers actually elected will be restricted to 120, with a further 120 nominated by

the statutory commission and the rest being allocated to political parties in proportion to the vote they achieve in general election. The seats occupied by bishops would be reduced from 25 to 16.

How much of the Lords should be appointed and what proportion elected? Wakeham suggested that 80% should be appointed, while a select committee sought to reduce this to 60%. Parliament was unable to agree on the percentage that should be elected and appointed, although the closest vote was linked to a proposal to elect 80% of the chamber. It is clear from polls that something like two thirds of the population want at least half the chamber elected, and almost the same number — three out of five — would like to see a chamber that was 80% elected. Unsurprisingly, the Lords took the view that the second chamber should be wholly appointed.

Freedom of information

The Freedom of Information Act was passed in 2000. It gives members of the public access to information held by public authorities, including the police, hospitals, companies and government departments. All public authorities have to produce a publication scheme, stating how they propose to deal with requests, how much they will charge and so on.

More than 100,000 bodies are covered by the legislation. A person has the right to request information from a public authority, and from January 2005 it became obligatory for the authority to provide this information within 20 days. But this has sometimes led to people being told within the 20 days that the information can only be provided if they wait for a much longer period. The Home Office took $8\frac{1}{2}$ months to refuse a request and apparently the Treasury has met the 20-day deadline in only 42% of cases. You can be charged for the information but the charge (£600 from central government, £450 for all other public authorities) is considered reasonable. In practice, most of the information has been given free of charge. Anyone can request this information and no reason has to be given as to why the information is required. All kinds of information have been released. Universities have been compelled to disclose links with arms companies, for example, and the Child Support Agency has to reveal the amount it pays to men wrongly accused of fathering children.

However, where such information is held to be prejudicial to national security or damaging to commercial and financial interests it can be legitimately withheld. An information commissioner has been appointed who can examine the case for exemptions where they have been contested.

Department for Constitutional Affairs

In 2003 a Constitutional Affairs Department was created to take responsibility for and consolidate the developments the government has made since 1997. The new department will concern itself with:

- justice
- rights
- democracy

In each of these areas the department will seek to improve the existing system and make it more transparent. For justice, the department wishes to establish a new tribunal system as well as offering guidance and information on how the current system works. The question of rights will be clarified, for example how they affect transsexual people, whose rights have suffered in the past. This area will embrace questions of electoral law and practice, and the issue of data protection.

As regards democracy, the department has the role of explaining the new system of devolution and coordinating the different parliaments and their work with Whitehall. It will provide information about the Lords reform; assist in the formation of joint ministerial committees to facilitate the work of devolved administrations; and offer advice and expertise on the role of the monarch and hereditary elements in British government today.

Summary

- Sovereignty is a problem for liberalism because it is usually attached to the state, and because the state uses force to tackle conflicts of interest it prevents people from governing their own lives.
- Liberalism prefers dispersal to concentration. As a result liberals often argue for federalism, but a federalist state still has the problem that afflicts all states: it uses force and hence can be said to undermine freedom.
- The UK has traditionally been relatively secure and self-confident, so it has not resorted to explicit nationalism to project itself. However, in 1997 New Labour decided to pursue policies of devolution and decentralisation out of fear that the insensitivities of the previous government had unwittingly strengthened minority nationalisms and insecurities.
- The devolution agenda granted an assembly for Wales and a parliament for Scotland. Nationalist parties in these areas have welcomed this, and these institutions have been coupled with mayoral elections in London and a willingness to take account of regional identities within England itself. Devolution in Northern Ireland has proved more difficult.

- Constitutional changes also embrace a new Human Rights Act; proposals to reform the House of Lords; a new Freedom of Information Act and the establishment of a Department of Constitutional Affairs.

Task 5.1

Read the passage below and answer the questions that follow.

Britishness and citizenship

In February 2004, 19 immigrants received British passports at a ceremony in which they took an oath of allegiance to the Queen as head of state. The Prince of Wales handed out certificates, congratulating those receiving them. 'Being British,' declared the Prince, 'is something of a blessing and a privilege for us all'. He hoped that the ceremony added something to the significance of acquiring British citizenship, and that 'it has reinforced your belief, if indeed any reinforcement is required, that you belong here and are very welcome'. He added that 'being a British citizen becomes a great source of pride and comfort for the rest of your life'.

Guardian journalists in September 2003 found that when they questioned nine British citizens about key aspects of British life, the average score was just 37%. Only a third of the sample could name the home secretary and knew what NHS Direct was, about 10% knew what the national minimum wage was, and none knew what the basic rate of income tax was.

Questions

1 How much history, and what kind, should a prospective citizen know about the UK?

2 Should prospective citizens have to swear allegiance to the British monarch even if they have reservations about the monarch's representativeness or legitimacy?

3 How important is a commitment to global values in prospective citizens?

4 How important is the notion of 'Britishness' and allegiance to the Union Jack?

5 Is English the same as British?

Guidance

Question 1

Most people agree that British citizens should be able to speak English. But is it necessary for a prospective citizen to have a historical knowledge about the UK? There are three problems here:

- Existing citizens may not know much about the UK's past and it seems unfair to demand knowledge from prospective citizens that existing citizens do not have.
- There is a problem with propaganda. Countries are often tempted to encourage a version of history that demonstrates their virtues and plays down abuses and negative events. Will those judging the citizenship credentials of candidates want a history that is anaemic and uncritical, so that the candidate demonstrates how splendidly the UK has acted in the past?

Task 5.1 (continued)

- Many of the applicants for citizenship come from countries in which the UK's involvement has been problematic. Will candidates be able to demonstrate the human rights abuses that have punctuated the UK's colonial past or will they simply tell adjudicators what they believe the adjudicators want to hear?

Question 2

This question is aggravated by the fact that many immigrants may even not be Christians, let alone Anglicans. Should they have to take an oath of allegiance to the head of state when such a person is bound by law to be an Anglican?

People applying for citizenship may feel ill at ease taking an oath to a head of state that can never adopt their own particular creed. What if prospective citizens are Jews, Catholics, Muslims, atheists, Hindus, Sikhs etc.? It is not a question of arguing that the monarch has to espouse the same belief system as they do, but if the monarch can *never* embrace their particular creed will this not dent the loyalty they are expected to show? The prospective citizen may be a republican. Will the demand for an oath to a monarch cause gratuitous offence? One might argue that if a person wants to be a citizen then an oath of allegiance to the head of state should be mandatory whoever the head of state is, but remember that it is in the UK's interest to have citizens who feel comfortable and secure in the country they have adopted.

Question 3

It is becoming increasingly clear that being a British citizen does not simply mean belonging to a particular country but having wider allegiances and values too. After all, prospective citizens need to be concerned with developments in the EU, so that they have a view of the relationship between being British and being a European. More and more legislation in the UK is linked to the EU, so it is vital that prospective citizens know something about the EU and how it is affecting the UK.

It is also important that would-be citizens feel that their destinies are linked to the fate of the world. The British media are full of debate about climate change and events abroad, and the reasons people apply to become British citizens are often connected to developments in the countries they are from. It is important that people see themselves not merely as British citizens, but in some sense as 'citizens of the world'. Many indigenous British people do not participate in politics and they may have a parochial view of the world. Tests for prospective citizens should encourage participation locally and regionally as well at the national and international level, so that a concern about world events is not seen as somehow 'disloyal' or dangerously cosmopolitan, but positive and necessary.

Becoming a British citizen is important, but people have many other identities and it is important that they retain and develop these as well.

Task 5.1 (continued)

Question 4

A number of immigrants have felt that the concept of Britishness excludes them and that the Union Jack is a symbol of the extreme right, rather than something with which they can identity.

It is important to be clear that while past identities and the actions of bigoted minorities should be noted, an independent attitude is crucial. The fact that the notion of Britishness and the display of the Union Jack have been (and are still in some quarters) used to promote exclusion and chauvinism does not mean that they are inherently exclusive and chauvinist. Being British can be seen as positive, and identified with attitudes and approaches that propagate toleration, unity and internationalism. The notion of Britishness is not static but continually changing, and prospective citizens should be made to feel that they are not joining a club with fixed rules, but becoming part of an entity that has as much to learn as it has to teach. The difference between assimilation and integration is that the former demands conformity to an existing identity while the latter encourages difference as well as unity, so that the would-be citizen is adding something to a changing cultural and political landscape.

Question 5

In continental Europe and the USA it is commonplace to refer to England as a synonym for the UK. There is a marvellous scene in the film *Tea with Mussolini* (1999) in which an Italian partisan calls out to troops 'Are you English?' 'No,' comes the reply, and the partisan's heart sinks since he imagines that the troops are German. 'We are not English, we are Scottish!' a sergeant major declares.

It is important that the UK is seen as a multi-national country. It is true that the majority of people in the UK are English, but this does not mean that the Scots, Welsh and Northern Irish should not see themselves as part of the UK as well. The same inclusiveness that relates to immigrants needs to be shown to the constituent nations of the UK, which have their own traditions and in some cases their own language. The government's system of devolution is an attempt to recognise this diversity and see it as positive. Unity and equality presuppose, and do not exclude, difference.

Task 5.2

Using this chapter and other resources available to you, answer the following questions:
1 Can liberalism handle the question of sovereignty?
2 Is devolution necessary in the UK?
3 Why did New Labour resort to devolution?

Task 5.2 (continued)

4 'The Human Rights Act is unnecessary and unworkable.' Discuss.

5 Do you see the Freedom of Information Act and the reform of the Lords as missed opportunities?

Guidance

Question 1

Liberalism is contradictory on this issue. On the one hand, it includes the important idea that the individual is sovereign. On the other hand, liberals see the state as sovereign as well, and postulate the idea that these two sovereignties are in harmony with one another, the individual's sovereignty contributing to, and forming the basis of, the sovereignty of the state.

But a moment's reflection demonstrates problems with this argument. If the state is an institution claiming a monopoly of force for a particular territory (Max Weber's definition, accepted by most liberals), then how can the use of force be reconciled with individual sovereignty? Not only does it seem odd to speak of members of a state as sovereign, since laws are passed that ultimately compel them to do things, but internationally states are constrained by treaties and international law. Can they still be called sovereign?

The term needs to be radically rethought so that (i) sovereignty is detached from the state — liberals are right to argue that the use of force is incompatible with freedom and sovereignty — and (ii) sovereignty does not mean doing as you please, but maximising your own capacity to govern your own life in a way that strengthens the capacity of others to govern theirs. Moreover, (iii) sovereignty is not only linked to individuals, and not something we either have or do not have. It is rather something towards which we move, while never actually exhausting the capacity to govern our own lives.

Question 2

It is sometimes argued that devolution represents a slippery road to disintegration. By recognising the existence of the Scots and the Welsh as distinct nations that are entitled to representation, the fear is that minority nationalisms will be encouraged and emboldened to press for outright secession. As regards Northern Ireland, it is argued that integration into the UK means the right to send representatives to the Westminster Parliament rather than seeking to create a power-sharing assembly in Belfast.

But the reality is that the UK is a multi-national country, and this reality is not going to disappear simply because it does not square with notions of a UK run from Westminster. Devolution should not be a dogma. If people do not want regional power, then it would be foolish to force it on them. A recent referendum in northeast

Chapter 5

Task 5.2 (continued)

England showed that people in that region felt regional government was unnecessary. But the situation is different in Scotland and Wales, where referendums indicated that a majority of people are in favour of devolved power. Note, however, that there is more enthusiasm for devolution in Scotland than in Wales, and that in Northern Ireland devolution has been complicated by the lack of trust between unionists and republicans. Nevertheless, it is hard to imagine a return to the kind of centralisation that characterised British politics before 1997.

Question 3

New Labour inherited social democratic policies that were in general favourable to liberalism. But it has given particular emphasis to this liberal heritage, and was conscious that the Labour movement in the past had been somewhat indifferent to constitutional change and the position of the individual.

The conservatives had pursued a policy of centralisation, and Labour felt that conservative attitudes towards the Scottish and the Welsh, among whom both Labour and the Liberals have traditionally drawn support, had strengthened nationalism. Contrary to the conservative claim that devolution augmented minority nationalisms, Labour argued that it was lack of devolution that exacerbated nationalist attitudes. The unity of the UK was threatened not by devolution, but by its absence, and Labour took the view that devolution would not strengthen nationalist attitudes, but actually undermine them.

Northern Ireland had shown that the neglect of minorities unwittingly boosts intransigent and extremist attitudes. In the same way, Scottish and Welsh nationalism was a punishment Westminster governments received for insensitivity and failure to reform. Hence New Labour embarked upon constitutional changes as a way of killing nationalism with kindness, and increasing the party's hold in areas where traditionally Labour and the Liberals had been strong.

Question 4

It is true that in the past the UK has relied upon common law — judgements delivered by the courts — to defend the rights of individuals, and the argument is that this piecemeal way of proceeding fits in well with British traditions. Passing an act that entrenches human rights is seen by some as un-British, and enshrining the European Convention of 1950 in British law demonstrates an unseemly reliance upon alien practices. The UK was a signatory to the convention: why does it need to incorporate it into its own legal system?

On the contrary, it could be argued that the UK has had landmark acts and declarations in the past in which citizens' rights have been secured. If the Human Rights Act (HRA) is un-British, then what are we to say about the Magna Carta and

Task 5.2 (continued)

the Bill of Rights (1688)? Human rights in the UK need a more comprehensive and systematic expression than the common law allows. There are all kinds of challenges today — one example is the effect of the environment upon individual wellbeing — that cannot be dealt with in the old way. Moreover, British interests can still be specifically protected by clauses in the act that allow governments to pass laws that contravene the HRA, provided of course that the 'incompatibility' is made explicit.

Question 5

The Freedom of Information Act gives members of the public (and of course the media) unprecedented power to probe and receive answers to questions that in the past could not have been raised. By insisting that only modest charges can be levied for information, and that 'public authorities' must reply within 20 days, new levels of transparency have been attained.

Reforms of the Lords have almost removed the hereditary element, and the appointment of new members must be undertaken by a commission which examines expertise, not party political credentials. Of these members, 20% will be appointed in this way, a further 20% will be elected and the rest of the new 600-strong chamber will be allocated according to party political strength in elections. The reduction of the number of bishops is surely in line with modernity, as is the development of a Supreme Court in contrast to the old system of Law Lords.

But it could be argued that public opinion in the UK seeks a predominantly elected second chamber. It is suspicious of 'appointments' and feels that removing the hereditary element requires a through democratisation. Like the Freedom of Information Act, too many concessions have been made to traditional interests, and paternalist attitudes have been allowed to persist.

Useful websites

- www.dca.gov.uk

Further reading

- Budge, I. (et al.) (2001) *The New British Politics*, Longman.

Chapter 6

Are we all liberals now?

It is sometimes argued that liberalism is so dominant in the West that we are all liberals now. Yet it is worth noting that liberalism has been criticised both by the left and the right, i.e. by those who feel that it does not go far enough, and those who believe that it goes too far.

The left — by which I mean social democracy, Marxism and anarchism — generally regards liberalism as unable to deal satisfactorily with the question of exploitation and emancipation. The right — by which I mean conservatism and fascism — sees liberalism as 'universalist' in character, and unable to handle questions of tradition and locality. In this chapter I will also make sense of what is often called 'postliberalism'.

Anarchism and Marxism

The notions of emancipation and self-government were initially raised by liberalism, and it has been pointed out that anarchism, although fiercely critical of liberalism, owes more to conventional liberalism than some of its exponents are willing to admit. The anarchist concept of the individual as a spontaneous actor derives from the classical liberal tradition.

Anarchists like William Godwin (1756–1836) in his *Enquiry Concerning Political Justice* (1793) not only supported utilitarianism, but spoke of the right individuals had to 'private judgement'. Anarchism, it could be asserted, takes the liberal argument that the state is artificial so seriously that it contends the state should not exist. Democratic socialists like Eduard Bernstein (1850–1932) saw socialism as 'organising liberalism', and social democrats have always acknowledged their indebtedness to liberalism.

Remember that Karl Marx (1818–1883) was steeped in liberal ideals, and in his early work he consciously identified with what he called 'the ever new philosophy of reason', characterising the state as the 'great organism' through which legal, moral and political freedom is realised. In the pages of the *Rhineland Gazette* Marx eloquently (if obscurely) champions the case for a free press, trial by jury and extended parliamentary representation.

The left's critique

The left complains that liberalism is abstract, and because it deals with individuals abstractly it is insufficiently inclusive. Feminists argue that traditional liberalism is male-oriented so that women are left out; Marxists see the working class and the poor generally as excluded, and anarchists have usually preferred the community to the market.

The authoritarian left has tended to use the term liberal pejoratively, as in Mao Zedong's (1893–1976) celebrated pamphlet 'Combat Liberalism', and the Stalinist tradition in particular has regarded liberalism as synonymous with decadence and exploitation. Whereas this section of the left has spoken approvingly of the notion of 'dictatorship', liberalism classically sees freedom and force as incompatible, and this seems to me a positive and valuable juxtaposition. The left's problem with liberalism is that it treats freedom and free will abstractly; Carole Pateman subtitles her book *The Problem of Political Obligation* (1985) 'a critique of liberal theory' because she asks: why should individuals who are 'naturally' free and equal have an obligation to obey the state?

Liberalism and the state

Rousseau took the view that under the state we are 'forced to be free', but this is generally regarded by other liberals as a rather shocking statement. Yet it could be argued that this is the implication of all liberal views, since liberals hold that somehow or other the state makes freedom and force compatible.

In his classic work *Liberalism* (1911), Hobhouse wrote of the 'self-governing state' without dwelling on the problem of how individuals coerced by the state can be said to govern their own lives. Pateman's point is that this voluntarism — the belief that the free will of the individual is unconstrained by circumstances — is not simply a conceptual position embraced by liberalism in the seventeenth and eighteenth centuries: it is basic to all liberal theory and is basic to liberal political theory today.

Pateman's argument is that to regard the state as 'natural' and 'unproblematic' conflicts with classical liberal principles, and reducing consent to voting in a liberal democracy is unsatisfactory. Hobbes's version of the social contract (although it has singular features) establishes a pattern followed by subsequent liberal theory. The individual is conceived as separate, self-contained and atom-like, and this is collectively expressed as the atomistic state sovereign whom individuals have to obey. The voluntarism is 'hypothetical' since liberalism cannot

practise what it preaches. There is a built-in conflict between liberal theory and oppressive practice.

Ethical vs economic liberalism

In his *Liberalism and Modern Society* (1992), Richard Bellamy distinguishes between 'ethical liberalism' and 'economic liberalism'. Ethical liberalism has an idealised view of the autonomous individual, while economic liberalism takes market-generated inequalities and a coercive state for granted. Bellamy's argument is that during periods of economic decline and social unrest, ethical liberalism is brushed aside and economic liberalism comes to the fore. With 'new liberalism' there is also great insistence on state intervention, and Hobhouse, Bellamy argues, is spared the potentially authoritarian implications of his theory until less prosperous times bring ethical and economic liberalism into conflict.

We have already spoken about Miliband's *The State in Capitalist Society* (see Chapter 4) and Macpherson's *The Life and Times of Liberal Democracy* (see Chapter 3); both complain that liberalism is the prisoner of the market and thus fails to practice what it preaches. Miliband and Macpherson accept liberal values, while providing a left-wing critique of contemporary liberal societies.

Carlyle's critique

The left is not alone in objecting to liberalism's support for the market and its tendency to abstraction. There is a fascinating review by the 24-year-old Friedrich Engels (1820–95) of Thomas Carlyle's (1795–1881) *Past and Present*, which Carlyle wrote in January 1844. Carlyle was a Tory and his book is a fierce critique of liberalism and the industrial revolution. As far as Carlyle was concerned, Chartism — a radical movement of the 1840s that campaigned for universal male suffrage — was a symptom of the

Thomas Carlyle

'condition of England' with its 'melancholy spectacle of a human being willing to labour but forced to starve.'

The Tories in the 1840s were generally opposed to what they saw as the doctrinaire harshness of the Whigs or liberals. Engels himself expressed a preference for the conservatives: 'a Whig would never have been able to write a book that was half so human as *Past and Present*.'

Carlyle's book draws upon the grim realities of the 1842 depression, in which 1 in every 11 of the population was out of work in England and Wales. In almost incendiary language, Carlyle depicts a country that has been bewitched so that poverty coexists with plenty, scarcity with abundance, and millions are confined to what he calls 'poor law Bastilles' (after the Liberals' Poor Law Amendment Act of 1834) — the workhouses.

One Betty Eules of Liverpool was hanged after poisoning her children and step-children, and Carlyle sees this tragedy as reflecting a doomed system that expresses both the myth of Midas (the king who turned to gold everything he touched) and the myth of the half-animal and half-woman Sphinx, the latter combining celestial beauty with a 'darkness, ferocity, fatality which are infernal'.

Carlyle describes how an all-pervasive alienation consigns society as a whole to atomised insecurity. The old theological Hell has given way to a new capitalist Hell — the hell of 'not succeeding, of not making money'. Rich mill owners hire their starving workers 'fairly' in the market. Carlyle relates how an Irish widow in Scotland expresses her unity with others by dying of typhus fever and fatally infecting 17 others in the process. 'Verily Mammon-worship is a melancholy creed,' he writes. Victorian capitalism is ridiculed by Carlyle as a system of 'shows and shams', and he sees elections as a great 'National Palaver': Chartism is the menacing shadow that will sweep such an edifice away.

Pantheism vs scepticism

Liberalism, in Carlyle's view, is an indulgent scepticism: 'All the Truth of this Universe is uncertain; only the profit and loss of it, the pudding and praise of it, are and remain very visible to the practical man.' What is the solution? Not 'Morrison pills', he argues (Morrison was a well-known quack of the 1820s), but a new aristocracy that will invite people to rediscover the 'eternal substance', the 'Bible of Universal History'. It is action, and work in particular, that resolves doubt — not money making.

Engels, who had just discovered the work of the German materialist Ludwig Feuerbach (1804–72) when he wrote his review, rejects Carlyle's pantheism (a belief that God is everywhere) — a position, Engels says, that prevents Carlyle from embracing 'a free and human point of view'.

The ambiguity of Engels's critique

Engels's review, though not uncritical, is extremely positive. A year after writing it, he describes Carlyle as having 'found the right path' and he hopes that Carlyle can follow it. Yet Carlyle's views are militantly right wing in character, and the problem of 'managing the working classes' falls to the captains of industry. These 'captains' are not motivated by profit, but by nobility and elitist ideals that make them leaders not merely of the nation but — because Carlyle approves of colonialism — of the world as well. If this is 'socialism', it has more in common with the 'socialism' of Adolph Hitler (1889–1945) than that of Karl Marx.

Friedrich Engels

Carlyle fiercely attacks democracy and despises the popular masses, but Engels sees this as merely a critique of 'bourgeois democracy'. He finds that although Carlyle lacks clarity about the goal and 'purpose of modern democracy', his account leaves 'little to be desired'. Because Carlyle is anti-liberal, Engels naively assumes he and Carlyle have much in common, and that Carlyle has only one more step to go before he sees the light! It is only later that Engels (with Marx in the *Communist Manifesto*, for example) sees the 'revolutionary' character of capitalism, historically speaking, and the dangers of a 'reactionary socialism' that hurls 'anathemas against liberalism'. Praise for Carlyle is omitted from later editions of Engels's *The Condition of the Working Class* (1845) and he is dismissed as a reactionary.

But Engels's review is revealing, particularly as it demonstrates the ambiguities of a left-wing position that is anti-liberal, and laced with romanticism and a kind of 'philosophical communism'.

Burke's critique

Liberalism is attacked from the right because of its universalism. The French Revolution in particular filled conservatives with alarm, and Edmund Burke warned against the dangers of the liberal vision. 'At the end of every vista,' he declared, 'you see nothing but gallows.' The notion that everyone is free and equal, endowed with natural rights by a benevolent deity, can only lead to a denial of tradition and diversity. It is experience, not abstract ideals, which must motivate us.

Burke is particularly hostile to abstraction. Abstraction leads to terror, and a belief in natural rights is no more than a dogma that stands in the way of respect for habit, taste and tradition. Burke defends what he calls 'prejudice' in the sense of 'pre-judgement' — an intuition as opposed to a fully developed rational argument. Pre-judgements are embodied in the wisdom of previous generations, and it is this wisdom that liberalism arrogantly rejects when it insists that thinking must start from 'first principles'. The notion of the state as a contract is an abstract dogma that ignores historical realities and the need for social hierarchy.

Rather than naively extol the 'people', Burke argues the case for guidance and leadership, and in his famous 'Speech to the Electors of Bristol' he contends that if local constituents have a hasty opinion, 'evidently opposite to the real good of the rest of the community', then their representative should decline to give it effect.

Unreal expectations and government by minority

Other conservatives, like Michael Oakeshott (1901–90), have warned against rationalism — the belief that, with reason, the thinker can sweep aside habit and tradition. Liberals create unreal expectations: principles of human rights, votes for women, the right of every nation to self-determination etc. A different kind of conservative critic of liberalism is Leo Strauss (1899–1973), who opposes the whole modernist tradition, going right back to Hobbes. Ironically, Strauss subscribes to the idea of natural rights, seeing it as an absolutist bulwark against relativism. He traces the notion back to the ancient Greeks and espouses a Platonic view: those with wisdom ought to rule.

Liberalism is vigorously and radically opposed by those on the extreme right too. There is an important tradition of elitism in Italian political thought, with Gaetano Mosca (1858–1941) arguing in *The Ruling Class* (1896) that all societies are governed by minorities, whether these be military, hereditary, priestly or based on merit or wealth. Mosca accepts that ownership of property can be a factor in accounting for elite rule, but he rejects the Marxist account that seeks to privilege this particular factor. The ruling class or elite owes its superiority to organisational skills, Mosca argues, and these alter according to circumstance. What he calls

the 'political formula' or the ideological mechanisms of rule vary, but all states are necessarily elitist in character, whether their legitimising myth be the divine right of kings, popular sovereignty or the dictatorship of the proletariat.

Democracy and the 'residues'

Democracy is simply, in the view of the elitists, a more subtle form of manipulation, and the parties offer inducements for people to vote for them. The 'political class' needs to be distinguished from other sections of the elite, like the industrialists, but in 1923 Mosca introduced the argument that elites can compete through rival political parties. People of lower socioeconomic origin are recruited in order to renew elites. Unlike other elitists, Mosca is fiercely critical of the Italian leader Benito Mussolini (1883–1945), and his critique of liberalism is best described as conservative rather than fascist.

Rather more hawkish is Vilfredo Pareto (1848–1923). In 1900 he declared himself an anti-democrat, arguing that the political movements in Italy and France were simply seeking to replace one elite with another. While he approves of Marx's emphasis upon struggle, he rejects completely the notion that a classless society is possible. As far as Pareto is concerned, human action is mostly non-logical in character, and stems from non-rational sentiments and impulses: what he calls underlying 'residues'. In his most important political and sociological work, *The Mind and Society* (1916), he distinguishes between Class I residues (inventive, imaginative capacities) and Class II residues (conservative, persistent tendencies).

Pareto argues that all government is government by an elite, which uses a combination of coercion and consent. Class I residues predominate when 'foxes' are in control — manipulative politicians who create consent — and Class II residues come to the fore when 'lions' are in control and violence is necessary. Each of these residues has its strengths and weaknesses, and the cycle of 'lions' replacing 'foxes' can be described as the 'circulation of elites'. Pareto saw Mussolini as a politician with a lion-like character who had displaced wily politicians.

Michels's iron law of oligarchy

Perhaps the most important figure of all when analysing the extreme right-wing critique of liberalism is the work of Robert Michels (1876–1936), a disillusioned German socialist who was greatly influenced by syndicalism, an anarchist belief that the revolt against capitalism must come from the trade unions.

In 1911 Michels published *Political Parties*. In it he argues that all societies and all organisations are subject to an 'iron law of oligarchy' (an oligarchy is a small group controlling the masses). Struck by what he saw as the contrast between the official statements of the German Social Democratic Party and the timidity of its political practice, Michels argues that oligarchy is present even in parties apparently committed to the norms of democracy. The fact that leaders are in practice autonomous from their followers derives from the constraints of organisation.

Although he wrote a good deal about psychology, Michels argues that oligarchical tendencies are based upon organisational rather than psychological factors. The complexity of organisations can only be grasped by professional leaders who have communication skills, and who understand the rules of elections and other external pressures. This leadership is made all the more entrenched by what Michels regards as the incompetence and emotional vulnerability of the masses.

He admired fascism and argues that, as with bolshevism, it is a reflection of the general tendency to oligarchy. Fascist political leaders, like Hitler, Mussolini and Oswald Mosley (1896–1980), rejected liberalism for its belief in reason, its notions of freedom and equality, and the cosmopolitanism of its ideals. The extreme right saw itself as revolutionary, and targeted liberalism as one of the sources of the 'decadence' it sought to erase.

The problem with (some) postmodernists

The prefix 'post-' has become fashionable as a result of the term 'postmodernism'. For some, 'post-' simply denotes a development that succeeds the original. According to this reading, fascism could be described as 'postliberalism' because it arose in the 1920s and liberalism has its roots in the seventeenth century.

In my view, however, this is an unsatisfactory interpretation of 'post-', since the latest version of a theory can always claim to be 'post-' the position it is criticising. I interpret 'post-' to imply a theory that *builds upon* (and does not simply reject) the body of thought it critiques. The problem with many self-styled postmodernists is that they do not go beyond modernism (by which I mean liberalism) but simply embrace positions of scepticism, nihilism and relativism, which are actually very old.

A postmodernist who argues, for example, that feminism cannot exist because women are all different and there is no such thing as a 'woman', effectively undermines the argument for women's rights. In this way, the challenge posed by the notions of freedom and equality that liberalism raises is merely brushed aside. Some postmodernists see the very idea of emancipation and self-government as arbitrary meta-narratives (i.e. stories that go beyond history), whereas it seems to me that concepts like emancipation and self-government, which we have inherited from the liberal tradition, should be made concrete and realistic.

It is one thing to criticise the abstract character of liberalism; it is quite another to go beyond these abstractions, so that the individuals we speak of are real life people and the concept of the individual embraces everyone. In other words, liberalism is both positive and negative, and postliberalism, as I interpret it, involves building upon the positive and jettisoning the negative.

Table 6.1 The two souls of liberalism

Positive features	Negative features
Everyone is free and equal	An abstract dictum that applies differently in practice
Everyone is an individual	Everyone owns themselves
Freedom is incompatible with force	An uncritical view of the state
People are able to govern their own lives	People must be ruled by repressive hierarchies
People have free will	People have to be governed by market relationships
We are all equal members of a global society	We are citizens of nation states
Everyone is different	Differences are threatening: equality can only mean that we are all the same

A defence of postliberalism

Postliberalism requires that we hold onto the positive features of the liberal tradition outlined in Table 6.1, and reject the negative ones. The assertion that everyone is free and equal is a powerful truth, but a number of points need to be made here.

First of all, everyone must really mean 'everyone', so if there are people who are left out, such as women, gays, black people etc., then it cannot be said that we are all free and equal. Historically, liberalism 'leaves out' whole categories of people, and its tendency to abstraction is rooted in the liberal belief that market relations are 'natural'. Everyone buys and sells things as abstract individuals, so we are deemed to be all the same and our real differences are concealed.

Second, we have to rethink our notions of freedom and equality. To be free is not to do as one pleases, but to *develop* oneself: to be equal is not to be the same as everyone else, but to enjoy the same rights, duties and respect. Of course, this notion of equality has enormous resource implications, since it is difficult for people to enjoy respect, for example, unless they are gainfully employed, can read and write, have good health etc.

A relational view

There is nothing wrong with the idea that we are all individuals. However, this statement must not only be interpreted inclusively, but in what I want to call a 'relational' way. By this I mean an understanding that our individuality is not a static property we inherit but the product of social relationships, and that our wellbeing as an individual depends upon, and can only be secured by, the wellbeing of other individuals. There is a marvellous example of relational thinking in a rural Zimbabwean greeting, where one person asks another if they slept well. Back comes the reply: 'I slept well if you slept well.' The wellbeing of each depends upon the wellbeing of the other.

Individuals do not 'own' themselves in the sense that they can do what they like with their bodies. Of course, every individual is entitled to privacy when they attend to their bodies, but this privacy is itself socially recognised. People have privacy to develop: one cannot be free (as John Stuart Mill pointed out) to destroy oneself. The idea that we are items of property with an absolute power over ourselves is a liberal prejudice that stems from a belief that humans are separate atoms unrelated to one another, governed only by market relations. Long after liberals abandoned the belief that individuals initially inhabit a state of nature, in which they forge a contract to form a society and a state, the concept of the abstract individual persists.

Once again…the problem of the state

Liberalism is correct to see force and freedom as incompatible, but this must mean that the state, as an institution that claims a monopoly of legitimate force, is a troubling and contradictory body. How can conflicts of interest be meaningfully settled if one party to a dispute is an enemy and has to be punished against their will?

Chapter 6

Conflicts can only be settled through negotiation, and arbitration (i.e. the use of social as opposed to 'statist' sanctions) requires a common interest between the parties that may sadly be absent. However, we should recognise (as I have already noted) that the use of force is dangerous and often counterproductive, and it can only be justified when it is used to make force redundant in the future. In other words, the force employed against a criminal should have the reduction (and ultimately elimination) of criminality as its objective, and this requires imaginative and enlightened ideas that do not simply blame the wrongdoer and demand that he or she be punished.

A different kind of utopianism

Surely a postliberalism that looks beyond the state is hopelessly fanciful and utopian. In my view, the positive features of liberalism, enshrined in the culture of liberal societies, are a powerful resource to build upon.

As I argued in *Beyond the State* (1995), we need to make a sharp distinction between government and the state. Governments resolve conflicts of interest through negotiation and compromise; the state tackles conflict through force. The liberal juxtaposition of force and freedom can only be meaningfully sustained if we develop a postliberal theory that looks beyond the state.

This involves gradually replacing the state with government (as defined above), not simply in one country but throughout the world. The destiny and wellbeing of all countries are interlinked, as environmental problems dramatically indicate. Wealthy countries have an interest in tackling the problems of poverty and war in poorer countries, since uncontrollable flows of refugees and immigrants to their own societies create problems, and generate attitudes that undermine a liberal political culture.

Increasing 'statism' makes it more difficult to handle cultural diversity in a democratic manner, and the problem of terrorism demonstrates graphically the interconnectedness of the globe. This is why the idea of looking beyond the state is both a utopian and a realist position to adopt.

A positive approach to liberalism

It has been frequently observed that liberalism is widely embraced in the West. Of course, different emphases prevail; conservatives prefer to stress the centrality of the market, whereas social democrats are more willing to regulate the economy and society through the state. In the USA (as is pointed out in the Introduction), liberalism has come to be used as a synonym for 'social' liberalism and even social democracy, so that conservatism is presented as a creed close to old-fashioned liberalism. It would seem odd in the USA to hear the Iraq conflict denounced as a product of liberalism, even though this is claimed frequently by European conservatives.

What are we to make of the hegemony of liberal values? Since the fall of communism, the domination of liberalism has increased. Francis Fukuyama (1952–) argues in his book *The End of History and the Last Man* (1992) that liberal democracy has become the unquestioned norm in all developed societies. It is important to take an attitude towards liberalism that is critical but also positive. We need to build upon the liberal tradition, extending rights and freedoms to parts of the population that liberalism itself has been unable to reach. This is why 'postliberalism' does not reject liberalism but seeks to go beyond it.

Conclusion

Liberalism is criticised by both the left and the right. Left-wing critics argue that liberalism does not and cannot practise what it preaches. Its notions of freedom and equality might be subversive, but they are also abstract, and have histori-cally ignored the needs of women, the poor, the dependent, workers and so on. Left-wing critiques sometimes reject all the values of liberalism, but even where they do not they complain that these values are institutionally expressed in an exclusive and partisan manner. Liberals normally approve of the market and a capitalist society, and their left-wing critics argue that these institutions generate the inequalities and abstractions that get in the way of emancipatory policies.

Of course, left-wing and right-wing criticisms share some common ground. Both complain about the hypocrisy of the liberal tradition and its abstract character. Some critiques appear ideologically ambiguous, but in my view the questions of equality, democracy and emancipation (at least as long-term objectives) differentiate right from left. Right-wing critiques see a need for natural hierarchies and regard liberalism as a soulless doctrine that undermines the importance of tradition, local identity and respect for nobility and greatness. The right sees the liberal notion of the individual as dangerously cosmopolitan and regards the belief in reason as naive and mechanistic. Conservative critiques stress the importance of continuity with the past; radical right-wing critiques emphasise the need to break sharply and totally with the egalitarian heritage of the European Enlightenment.

It is important, in my view, to build upon rather than simply push aside liberal values. Hence I make the case for a postliberalism that accepts the positive features of liberalism while dispensing with the negative ones. This means that the liberal opposition to force is utilised to make a critique of the

state that is realistic and convincingly demonstrates that the state itself is a barrier to freedom, equality and emancipation.

It is true that liberalism has become the overarching norm of western societies. This is a good thing, provided we demand that liberals practise what they preach, and become postliberals as a consequence.

Summary

- When examining the left-wing critique of liberalism, it is worth noting that both anarchism and Marxism are greatly in its debt. Yet the left takes the view that liberalism excludes vulnerable people who do not flourish in market-based societies. Liberalism, the left contends, has an abstract and unsatisfactory notion of freedom.
- Liberalism juxtaposes freedom and force while supporting the need for a state. This inconsistency is inherent in all forms of liberalism. Even the new liberals are unable to reconcile their ethical principles with a belief that the market is natural and necessary.
- Engels's youthful critique of Carlyle demonstrates the ideological ambiguity between left and right, and the ease with which an attack on liberalism can be applauded even though such an attack seeks to replace liberal institutions with elitist and authoritarian ones.
- Conservatives reject liberalism on the grounds that it takes insufficient account of tradition and subscribes to a naive belief that all are rational, free and equal. A more extreme rejection of liberalism is presented by fascists, who display contempt for democracy and take the view that all societies are governed by elites.
- Some postmodernists simply reject liberalism, whereas the challenge is to build upon its strengths while jettisoning its weaknesses. A relational approach is required so that we can develop a postliberalism that looks beyond the state and pushes liberalism into spheres it has traditionally ignored.
- Liberalism is hugely influential in contemporary Western societies. It moulds the value systems of conservatives and socialists, as well as those who designate themselves as liberals.

Task 6.1

Read the following quotation from the National Front's website and answer the questions that follow.

> The National Front's policies and principles stem from a fundamental belief in the right of individuals to determine their own future and the future of their community to the greatest possible limits. Real political and economic power has progressively been taken away from the British people and a new Class

Task 6.1 (continued)

Politique has developed which takes an ever-increasing range of decisions without reference to the wishes of the people.

Britain's political system has been described as an 'elective dictatorship' with the government able to push through a whole range of policies, claiming a 5 year mandate on the basis of a general election where usually only about 30–40% of the voting population have given one party a parliamentary majority.

In fact, as far as a whole range of issues are concerned, the electorate has been given precious little alternative. On issues such as European integration, capital punishment, immigration, international free trade, Northern Ireland etc. there is very little difference between the three old parties.

These three parties exercise a stranglehold over British politics with support from the media, large parts of which are actively hostile to any new radical party of nationalism. In Britain and in other European nations the Class Politique now regards itself as the natural rulers, able to ignore and reject the views and wishes of the majority of the people on the basis that 'They know best' — such arrogance is usually a sign of imminent destruction.

Questions for discussion

1 The National Front (NF) sees differences — people with different cultures and appearances — as threatening and contaminating. Is it right to assume that white Britons are a homogenous bloc?

2 The NF assumes that national identity overrides other identities. What about the fact that we are men or women, scientists or artists, northerners or southerners, Catholics, Protestants or atheists etc.?

3 Is it meaningful to simply reject the trend to large-scale economic and social units? Are 'Europeanisation' and globalisation merely mistakes — a trend to be reversed? Can you have an emancipatory socialism if liberal values are despised and denigrated?

Task 6.2

Using this chapter and other resources available to you, answer the following questions:

1 Do you agree with the proposition that we are all liberals now?

2 Why do the critics of liberalism focus upon the question of abstraction?

3 What differentiates the right-wing and left-wing critics of liberalism?

4 How effective is the conservative critique of liberalism?

5 'All opponents of liberalism necessarily espouse some kind of authoritarianism.' Do you agree?

Chapter 6

Task 6.2 (continued)

Guidance

Question 1

Liberal values are extremely influential in the UK and throughout western Europe. This is as it should be, since people increasingly see themselves as individuals entitled to enjoy freedom, respect from others, and have a private life. Admittedly not everyone pursues values that accord with the liberal tradition. But customs that are not liberal can be tolerated where they do not harm others, and are not imposed through violence.

But, although it is influential, liberalism has its problems, and many are seeking to go beyond liberalism in a way that preserves what is positive in the liberal tradition and discards what is negative. Liberalism has placed the market at the centre of its values. Yet challenges are building up — in transport, energy supplies and the environment, to name just three — which arguably require solutions involving public activity that will 'interfere' with the unconstrained choices of individuals. The market might dictate a situation in which the economic divide within and between countries increases. But will this not undermine democracy? Indeed, it could be argued that liberalism itself will be in jeopardy unless we adopt policies of a 'postliberal' character — moving towards consensus, negotiation and international coordination.

Question 2

Critics of liberalism, from both the right and the left, see liberal values in general and the market in particular as lacking concreteness. Both argue that there is an absence of stress upon tradition and development; a belief that the individual is somehow outside of or more important than society; and that the market encourages a freedom and equality in which real differences are concealed behind transactions. Money becomes a substitute for quality, and luck and fortune take the place of hard work and merit.

That said, liberalism's critics draw different conclusions from their critique of abstraction. Right-wing critics see in abstraction a dangerous tendency to conceal hierarchies of gender and class. The market is a wicked institution because it enables women and relatively poor people to become successful and upset traditional institutions. It allows minorities such as Jews, black people, atheists and gays to promote their values, and free trade promotes a cosmopolitanism that undermines national identity and greatness.

Left-wing critics attack abstraction for diametrically opposed reasons. They complain that the market offers a freedom and equality that is too formal and superficial. Because it ignores the real disparities in wealth and power, freedom is negatively conceived and equality can be illusory. Liberal abstractions are, however, an

Task 6.2 (continued)

opportunity to demand reform and transformation, so that the market is an important advance even if it is increasingly inadequate as a way of addressing social problems.

Question 3

Left-wing critics focus on the need to move beyond liberalism, whereas right-wing critics regard liberalism as a betrayal of eternal values that should not be tampered with. Liberalism introduced concepts of self-government, emancipation, freedom and equality into political discourse. For the right, these notions are inherently suspect. They encourage anarchy: how can the need for guidance and leadership be reconciled with self-government, equality between the sexes, and a belief that people should be able to do as they please?

Certain strains of left-wing criticism have echoed these positions and adopted anti-liberal postures that have led to the violation of human rights and a menacing authoritarianism. Stalinism and Maoism, for example, though doctrines of the left, have attacked liberalism in ways that have strengthened autocratic and undemocratic rule. This has helped to create the argument that both left and right are opposed to democracy and individual rights.

On the other hand, the democratic left criticises liberalism because it traditionally leaves out whole categories of people — women, the poor and ethnic minorities — and has notions of freedom and equality that are negative and abstract. The repressive hierarchies that are banished through the front door come slithering in through the back. It is not that liberalism is wicked; it is that it is inadequate and inconsistent. It suffers from a gulf between theory and practice that can only rectified if the liberal tradition is built upon in creative, socially conscious and innovative ways.

Question 4

The conservative critique of liberalism is effective in its attack on abstraction. Tradition is important. So is custom and continuity with the past. People live in society and need to recognise and respect others. Nor should we imagine that people are the same: people have different values and customs, and we should not assume that we have all the answers and others have none. Conservatism emphasises the importance of locality and region: local institutions may not fit in with rational schemes that are imposed from above, but where they 'work' they should be left alone.

Where the conservative critique of liberalism runs into difficulty is in the solutions it proposes. Conservatives often want to go backwards, idealising the past and ignoring the fact that traditional institutions have been undermined precisely because they have failed to meet popular needs. People have become less and less inclined simply to do what they are told. Conservative attempts to revive past notions of heroism and

Task 6.2 (continued)

methods of rule seem archaic and unworkable, and instead of condemning liberalism for encouraging greater equality and democracy they should be praising it for this and criticising it only for its inconsistency and hypocrisy in this regard.

Question 5

Critics of liberalism can easily reject, rather than build upon, liberal values. When they do so, they inevitably espouse authoritarian institutions and attitudes that seem part of a common totality. It is said, for example, that Hitler was a great admirer of Stalin and planned to allow Stalin to continue to rule over a USSR brought under Nazi control. Georges Sorel (1847–1922), whose theories of myth were influential among fascists, greatly admired Lenin for his firm rule. So there is something in the argument that the critics of liberalism espouse authoritarianism.

But if this argument is partly true, it is also partly false, since it assumes that a critic of liberalism must reject liberal values. But why should the critic not challenge liberalism to practise what it preaches? If force is incompatible with freedom, why should we regard the state as a permanent part of the political landscape? If freedom is important, then it should be translated into real power and material resources — how can people be said to be equal when one is rich and the other poor? If men are rational individuals, why can't women be as well? These, and many similar questions, can be raised by those critics of liberalism who do not see authoritarianism and repression as the way forward.

Useful websites

- www.en.wikipedia.org/wiki/Liberalism

Further reading

- Burke, E. *Reflections on the Revolution in France.*
- Carlyle, T. *Past and Present.*
- Hoffman, J. and Graham, P. (2006) *Introduction to Political Ideologies*, Pearson Longman.

Conclusion

Liberalism is an ideology in that it embraces a number of political beliefs and focuses on the state. It is an extremely heterogeneous doctrine, and liberals of different persuasions have conducted fierce arguments among themselves.

Classical liberalism arose in the seventeenth century and roots its arguments for individual freedom and equality in the notion of a state of nature, in which people are conceived as initially existing outside of society and in a stateless condition. This view represents a sharp break from ancient and medieval thought, since it holds that hierarchy is unnatural and the formation of the state a purely conventional or artificial process. Note that the character of this state of nature differs significantly from liberal to liberal.

Hobbes, Locke and Rousseau

Hobbes sees the state of nature as a destructive war of all against all; Locke, on the other hand, depicts it as a much more peaceable process governed by natural law; while Rousseau seeks to avoid anachronism by presenting humans in the state of nature as little more than animals.

Nevertheless, all classical liberals regard the state as the product of contract. Although Hobbes argues the case for a powerful sovereign state his premises were distrusted by royalists during the Civil War, and there is a compelling case, in my view, for regarding Hobbes as the founder of liberalism.

The utilitarians

In the eighteenth and nineteenth centuries the notion of a state of nature was discarded, with liberals arguing that humans are social creatures and the state is not the result of a social contract. Liberals of the Scottish Enlightenment, like Hume and Smith, continue to champion the 'natural' character of commerce and trade, while the utilitarians express what their critics see as a quintessentially

bourgeois view, arguing that while the notion of natural right is redundant, all individuals pursue pleasure and avoid pain.

Even though utilitarianism was modified by John Stuart Mill so as to differentiate between higher and lower pleasures, liberalism still focused on the individual in an abstract way. The new or social liberals began, however, to contend that state intervention could be justified and that capitalism would only appeal to the masses if real social reforms were implemented.

Democracy

Social liberalism itself provoked a reaction in the form of what is usually called 'neoliberalism', a doctrine that believes in the sanctity of markets, but combines this with a suspicious attitude towards equality. Neoliberals also raise traditional liberal reservations about democracy.

Although liberalism is often treated as though it is a synonym for democracy, in fact liberals are historically opposed to it. They argue that democratic societies are unstable and subject to mob rule; indeed, this view is put by the Federalists influential in the formation of the US Constitution. The truth is that even Jefferson is best described as a liberal republican rather than as a democrat. Until the US civil war, democracy is seen as just one element in the Constitution, and Tocqueville's famous study of US democracy in the 1840s is really an analysis of a liberal society with an unusually broad spread of property ownership.

Voting and participation

British liberals like James Mill and Bentham began to make a cautious case for male universal suffrage, and it is easy to forget that although John Stuart Mill is concerned about the position of women and the poor, he is wary of democracy. It is only after the First World War that democracy is praised by liberals as a 'good thing', and after the Second World War a 'realist' theory of politics developed that sees democracy as a system in which politicians make decisions, while the popular masses confine themselves to voting for competing elites.

When considering whether and to what extent the UK is a liberal democracy, it is worth noting that critics like Miliband and Macpherson have argued that in capitalist societies power is much more concentrated than it appears. Although liberal institutions are desirable, they are emasculated by capitalist power. Macpherson takes the view that the vicious circle between apathy and inequality can be broken by a more participatory model that could preserve the party system.

The problem of inequality

Inequality is a real problem for a liberal democracy, and the electoral and parliamentary systems in the UK arguably weaken its democratic character. Its involvement in Northern Ireland and Iraq has strengthened the secretive nature of the British state, even though Europhiles see membership of the European Union as a factor boosting the UK's democratic institutions. Those who see democracy as a 'tyranny of the majority' blame it for what is in fact a problem with the state.

Devolution and constitutional change

The concept of sovereignty is a problem for liberal theory. The liberal preference for federalism might attempt to spread power, but this coexists with support for an institution that claims a monopoly of legitimate force for a particular territory. Traditionally the UK has been defended as a unitary state, but New Labour has embraced the liberal agenda of devolution for Scotland and Wales, and, with much more difficulty, for Northern Ireland as well.

New Labour has introduced a Human Rights Act, so that human rights arise not merely from the common law but are more systematically formulated, as the 1950 European Convention becomes part of British law. The Freedom of Information Act has extended the rights of British citizens, and reform of the House of Lords, though often criticised for being overly cautious, represents an attempt to bring the second chamber into the twenty-first century.

The critique of liberalism

The idea that we are all liberals now must take account of left- and right-wing critiques of liberalism. Left-wing critics argue that liberalism does not and cannot practise what it preaches. Although liberal notions of freedom and equality challenge the 'natural' hierarchies enshrined in ancient and medieval thought, there is a divide between theory and practice. Historically such concepts have ignored women, the poor, the dependent, workers etc., so that left-wing thought is invariably concerned with the wellbeing of those left out in the cold.

Of course, it is possible for left-wing ideologies to reject rather than go beyond liberal values (think of Stalinism, Maoism, Leninism and arguably anarchism), but all left-wing critiques take the view that liberalism is exclusive, and despite its claims to universality see liberalism as partisan in its interests and concerns. Liberals normally support capitalism and the market, institutions that left-wing critics regard as creating the kind of inequality that divides people and creates conditions for strife and war.

This is not to deny the liberal charge that left-wing and right-wing criticisms share some common ground. Both complain about the hypocrisy of the liberal tradition and its abstract character. Indeed, it might be difficult to decide whether a regime, ideology or critique is left wing or right wing (e.g. Colonel Gadaffi's Libya), but in my view, left-wing ideologies aim to achieve equality and emancipation in some timescale or other.

Right-wing critiques challenge the notion of equality, arguing that people are 'naturally' divided according to ethnicity, religion, gender etc. They regard liberalism as a sceptical doctrine that undermines the importance of tradition, local identity and 'instinct'. Whereas left-wing critiques usually applaud internationalism, right-wing critiques oppose it; whereas left-wing critiques seek to make reason 'concrete', right-wing theories reject it altogether. Conservatives complain that liberalism ignores the importance of continuity with the past; radical right-wing critiques emphasise the need to break sharply and totally with the idea of human rights, emancipation and freedom as universal values.

Postliberalism

As I see it, it is crucial not to throw the baby out with the bathwater. We should build upon rather than simply reject liberal values, and postliberalism is presented as a standpoint that accepts the positive features of liberalism while dispensing with the negative ones. The idea that people can govern their own lives and are rational, free and equal is central to a theory of emancipation, even if this means that liberal opposition to force must become the basis for a theory that looks beyond the state.

Liberalism can be realised if we reinterpret its notion of freedom and challenge the need to tackle conflicts of interest through an institution that divides humanity and normalises the use of force.